Advance Reviews

"No Time Marketing is a quick, effective way to dramatically boost the effectiveness of you company's marketing efforts. If you want to create a well-thought-out marketing plan that will work this is the book for you."

Brian Lawley
Author, "Expert Product Management"
Former President, Silicon Valley Product Mgt. Association

"In supporting hundreds of very smart women business leaders, we hear so often that they urgently need marketing help. In this day and age when every expense must be justified, No Time Marketing explicitly identifies what works and what doesn't. Even experienced marketers can learn some great tips and important ideas from the book."

Aileen Gorman
Executive Director, The Commonwealth Institute

"As the founder of the nation's largest marketing agency, I can tell you that every small to medium size company should have this book on their shelf, and it should be dog-eared."

Jack Sims
Speaker on Attainable, Sustainable Business Growth, If you think you know business and brand growth ... you don't know Jack!

"Make Time for No Time Marketing! Alyssa Dver is a wealth of knowledge and this book is a MUST!"

Ja-Naé Duane
President & Founder, Wild Women Entrepreneurs

"No Time Marketing is packed full of valuable marketing advice. Companies of all sizes will benefit from the myriad of smart, practical ideas to take their businesses to the next level."

Lynn Toomey
Chief Creativity Officer, Let's Gogh Marketing
Leader, Ladies Who Launch

"Not sure whether your current marketing plan is getting the most bang for the buck? No Time Marketing is your company's new marketing plan. Spend just one day working through the book or break it up into a few 30-minute working sessions and you'll have an action-oriented, easily executable, profit-focused marketing plan within a few hours."

Diane K. Danielson
Founder & CEO, DowntownWomensClub.com

"For many of us, marketing can be an elusive concept—we know we need it, but not sure what to do first. This book debunks traditional thinking and sheds light on real applications that work to determine how best to connect with your customers to generate real sales leads and ultimately, real revenues."

Victoria Colligan
Founder and CEO, Ladies Who Launch

"No Time Marketing" is an invaluable treasure chest of tips and tactics any company should open and use to increase marketing efficiency and "time to value." Of particular note are the integrated templates that enable you to not only learn and think about what you need to do, but to simultaneously build an action plan of "to dos" and next steps so you can execute. Highly, highly recommended.

Rick Chapman
Managing Editor & Publisher, *Softletter,* **Author,** *The Product Marketing Handbook for Software* **and** *In Search of Stupidity: Over 20 Years of High-Tech Marketing Disasters*

No Time™
Marketing

Small Business-Sized Steps in 30 Minutes or Less

Alyssa S. Dver

Meghan-Kiffer Press
Tampa, Florida, USA
www.mkpress.com
Innovation at the Intersection of Business and Technology

Publisher's Cataloging-in-Publication Data

Dver, Alyssa.
No Time Marketing
p. cm.
Includes appendices and index.
ISBN-10: 0-929652-47-9 (paperback : alk. paper)
ISBN-13: 978-0-929652-47-4 (paperback : alk. paper)
1. Marketing - Management 2. Small business – Marketing 3. New products - Marketing. I. Dver, Alyssa. II Title

HF5451.M374 2009   Library of Congress Control Number: 2008942444
005.3'068'8–dc21 Dver   CIP

Book's Website: http://www.NoTimeMarketing.com

Published by
Meghan-Kiffer Press
310 East Fern Street — Suite G
Tampa, FL 33604 USA

Company and product names mentioned herein are the trademarks or registered trademarks of their respective owners.

Meghan-Kiffer Press books are available at special quantity discounts for corporate education and training use. For more information write Special Sales, Meghan-Kiffer Press, Suite G, 310 East Fern Street, Tampa, Florida 33604 or email info@mkpress.com or call (813) 251-5531.

Meghan-Kiffer Press
Innovation at the Intersection of Business and Technology
Tampa, Florida, USA

Printed in the United States of America.   SAN 249-79

Dedication

This book is dedicated to all the brave entrepreneurial men and women who sacrifice their egos, income, and sleep because they refuse to just consume. I hope this book improves their businesses and inspires them to tackle whatever challenges lay between this moment and their dreams.

Thank you to my husband, Jeff, for his ever-patient support. Finally, to my two sons, Zack and Ben, who are my 'bookends' that perpetually snuggle me with joy and purpose.

Table of Contents

Introduction

Pedantic? *Perhaps.* Practical? *Absolutely.*

If you teach or revere marketing theory, you're going to detest this book. If you are an over-subscribed, over-stressed and under-budgeted business person, I believe that you will love it.

Whether you work for an existing business or are just starting one, I bet you need some marketing help. People say they can never have too much money or fame, and usually you only get those with marketing. So my assumption is that you are reading this to increase your marketing knowledge and effectiveness. If you work in a small or midsize business, you probably have little money, less time, and absolutely no patience for anything except positive results.

Speaking about a lack of patience, go ahead and admit it. Much of the time, we all suffer from Attention Deficit Disorder (ADD). With no time to spare, we are so overwhelmed with the mere thought of being busy, that we often can't think straight.

Ourselves, our customers, our colleagues, our prospects – no one has time to market or be marketed to.

And adding insult to injury, technology has made marketing even more challenging: TiVo, blogs, social networks, spam filters, callerID – all are designed to "save" us time and shield us from wicked marketers.

Lastly, as responsible business people, we are also under more scrutiny to quantitatively measure marketing. No wonder we are obsessed with quantitative but often superficial metrics such as clicks per page, downloads per day, or Google, Digg, Technorati, or Alexa rankings.

While most people think they can be marketers, ("I consume, therefore I can market") the reality is that good marketing was never easy—and it's getting pretty darn impossible. More formats and channels are available making it harder to get and keep a targeted attention.

> ***Successful marketing used to be a matter of creativity.***
> ***Today, it's a matter of precision.***

Ironically, there has never been a time when understanding marketing fundamentals was more important than it is today.

My mission with this book is to unspin the mysteries of marketing quickly, without insulting your intelligence. *This is not marketing for dummies.* It is marketing for really smart people who don't have the time, money, or perhaps the experience to do marketing—but they clearly know that they need it desperately. Alternatively, if you want to hire a marketing person (as an employee or as a consultant), this book should help you validate his or her knowledge and modus operandi (M.O.) so that you can invest in a marketing expert who will generate business and not just noise.

The first and most crucial part of any marketing plan is to confirm who your customers are and why they buy your products or services – or why they buy something else or simply live without your products or services. Learning these things is easier said than done, so this book aims to help. I'll pinpoint the critical strategic questions you should ask before making any marketing decisions. For those questions that you can't answer, I'll guide you to find the answers. With the right information, you'll quickly build an actionable marketing plan that includes short term tactics. Beyond that, I'll help you consider the longer term issues that you need to consider once you have obtained your new marketing smarts.

I know that you are too busy to read a lot and you are definitely too busy to ponder fancy charts and graphs. Therefore, in the following pages, I will cut to the chase and not fill you up with my own marketing stories and other companies' case studies. I will instead give you quick ways to establish a sound marketing plan that can put it into action immediately. The goal is to help you identify and leverage opportunities so you can sell more *stuff* and make more *money*. Okay with you?

Here's the drill: Each of the following eight steps includes "**No Time**™ **To-Do's**" that take 30 minutes or less to complete. They'll help you develop and implement a solid, defendable, and measurable marketing plan that is specific for your business.

Step 1. We'll do a marketing inventory to assess what critical information you already know and what you need to find out.

Step 2: We'll put a plan into place to fill in the missing blanks from your marketing inventory to ensure that you have all the information needed to make smart marketing decisions.

Step 3: We'll use the information from the marketing inventory and create a powerful positioning and messaging framework.

Step 4: We'll create (or validate) your pricing strategy.

Step 5: We'll build a plan to acquire new leads by pushing your message out to the specific places where your prospects are paying attention. We'll do this by opening the treasure chest of marketing tools to help you select the most cost effective tactics that can best work in your specific market with your specific target prospects. And then most importantly, we'll determine how to track your programs to make sure that they deliver the necessary results!

Step 6: We'll select the materials and programs that are needed to foster leads and pull those prospects closer to a successful purchase decision.

Step 7: We'll validate your marketing plan and business assumptions easily without writing a long, formal document.

Step 8: We'll look at ways to refine the plan over time to keep it accurate and effective.

You don't have to do all of the steps all at once and, in fact, you can't. You have other things to tend to in your business and some of the steps rely on feedback from other people who will respond based on their own schedule.

Reserve 30 minutes per week or even per month if that is all you can do. At least you'll be moving toward having a realistic marketing plan and you'll know how to start and when to end. The reality is that no marketing plan is perfect, and it is something that evolves over time as we continue to learn more about our products, customers, and ever-changing world. As such, we will focus on the salient issues and accept the fact that, given the constraints of the real world, it's certainly better to do our best and make refinements over time than doing nothing at all.

So, without taking any more of your very precious time and attention, start the clock – in *no time*, you will be well on your way to having an effective marketing plan.

Sales. Period.

Chapter 1:
Why Bother Marketing?

Whether it's an existing business or a brand new one, marketing can help salespeople and the sales process be more productive – that is, to sell more and to sell more quickly. Thus, marketing can reduce the cost of sales and optimize margins.

But marketing is often hard to measure and justify on its own. Much of the marketing done today is, "because we always did it that way," or "because our competitors do it that way," or "because we can't afford to do anything else." Obviously, these are not very strategic approaches and, quite frankly, they are irresponsible.

It is no surprise then that when sales are down, marketing is usually the first budget cut. It's easy to cut any budget when there isn't a clear tie to revenues and when the marketing plans are not defendable. In this book, we will use revenue generation as our marketing ruler - both as a measure and as a master. If your company doesn't see a measurable increase in sales, you should indeed question the applied marketing initiatives – and associated budget. Your company doesn't have the luxury of time or money to do creative work for the sake of art. In short:

> **The Marketing Golden Rule:**
> Marketing dollars spent must generate clear sales results.

In smaller businesses, it is not uncommon that sales and marketing are one and the same. Cold calling is marketing. Lining up reference sites is a part of marketing. Filling in Request for

Proposals (RFPs) and making brochures, websites, direct mail pieces, and other sales tools are all part of marketing. Essentially everything in the sales cycle except negotiating the deal and taking the order is usually considered part of the marketing function.

In larger organizations, the marketing function may be amorphous even when a "marketing department" exists. Split among groups such as sales operations, pre-sales support, marketing communications and others, it is easy to find many different objectives and perspectives about how marketing works in a given company.

If you ever took a formal marketing class or read an academic book on marketing, you are most likely familiar with the 4 P's of Marketing: Product, Price, Promotion, and Place (distribution or channel). Strangely, the one P that is absent is possibly the most important: *the PURCHASER!* If we don't know intimately about this P, marketing can become academic, expensive, and irrelevant.

A Practical Marketing Definition

> *Marketing identifies, attracts, fosters and retains*
> *qualified sales leads.*

Often marketing expenses are excused for the sake of the brand, for sales support, or to ensure customer retention. I submit that any marketing must justify its expense (time and money) by generating qualified leads into the sales process.

Generating Qualified Leads

In Chapter 6, we'll talk about obtaining leads and then in Chapter 7, we'll talk more about fostering leads and the critical ability to track leads. For the meantime, let's consider a lead as a person or business that has the ability and potential need to purchase your products or services. "Ability" includes the money (or other bartering assets) and other relevant factors that allow a prospect to understand and use your offering. A "potential need" means that prospects may or may not know that they have any problem (a.k.a. a latent need) or they may be unaware that there is any solution that exists to address their problem. Part of the marketing challenge is to educate such potential buyers so they feel the "pain" of not having your solution. The lead may be the potential buyer or actual user. They may influence the buying decision and, in fact, may not be a single person but instead a committee or group of individuals assigned to the purchasing decision. In the end, a qualified lead is the person or group that will make the decision to purchase the product or service and those who will be influential in the purchasing process.

In the process of qualifying a lead, you may find that a person is an influencer in the buying process and not the actual decision maker. Qualification may expose that the prospect is interested but not currently funded, though could be in the future. All such information is critical in the process of identifying, attracting, and fostering the right leads that can be transformed into successful sales.

Leads can come from multiple sources such as lists you purchase, trade shows you attend, or from inquiries coming in from your website. Leads may be prospective customers or they may be existing customers that want to buy again or buy additional different offerings from you than they did previously. It is often said that existing customers are your best leads since they already know about your company and ought to have a positive impression if they bought from you before.

Think through the upside potential of selling to an existing customer versus a new one. Assess whether a new customer sale or existing customer sale will be more profitable to your business. Consider both the profit in terms of dollars but also intangible factors such as reputation and references that can benefit your business and future sales. While you may want to sell to both existing customers and new prospects, make sure that you have enough resources (time, money, and talent) allocated to do both well.

> ⊘ **No Time**
> **NO-NO**

Many people think generating as many leads as possible is the objective. However, if you generate leads that aren't qualified, you can waste your company's very valuable time and money to find out that a prospect isn't even capable of purchasing your offering. Too many leads and you won't be able to follow up properly. This may leave qualified leads thinking that your company isn't responsive. You do, however, need to generate enough leads to allow for the inevitable sales situations – sales cycles that take longer than others, prospect budgets or organizations that change unexpectedly, or changes in your own budget and organization. Business isn't always predictable so it's always necessary to generate more leads than sales deals expected.

So how many leads are enough? In more sophisticated marketing discussions, the number of leads needed is measured against the rate at which the sales department closes leads into deals. For example, sales may have historically closed one out of every ten qualified leads. This "close rate" helps determine how many leads are needed to reach desired sales goals. In our example, if your salespeople need to close 10 deals to make their target revenues, they will need 100 leads (10:1). For our purposes in this book however, we will consider this type of lead forecast exercise an analytical luxury for most companies and therefore assume that you need to generate "a lot" of leads immediately. Having too many leads may cause business growth challenges, but I personally prefer that challenge rather than having the problems that are caused by too few leads. The main caveat with generating too many leads is being able to follow up on the leads effectively.

⊘ **No Time**
NO-NO

There is no point in getting leads that get stale, or worse yet, disappointing prospects by your company's inability to respond. So a better metric for determining how many leads you need to generate may be simply the number of leads that your organization can properly handle.

Push and Pull Marketing

Two common concepts used in marketing are: *push* (identify and attract) and *pull* (foster and retain).

Push marketing means that you go out and find prospects to buy your products or services. Once they know about you, pull marketing is what you do to get them to purchase your product or service. You need to do both to attract and catch as many fish as possible with your marketing net.

To find prospects you can purchase lists, attend trade shows, send out mailings, create search engine keywords, and do other proactive targeting activities. In the best case, prospects find out about your products and services from a trusted relationship – a referral. (We'll talk more about push methods in Chapter 6.) As a marketer, you are pushing information to them to make them aware of and interested in your offerings. Without the push approach, prospects may never know of their "need" or of your solution. But pushing information is a tough proposition in today's Opt-In, SPAM/CANN-restricted universe. Certain types of advertising and other 'passive' means such as free trials and sponsored events can be ways to bring new products or services to your prospects' attention, even if they weren't specifically looking for them. You may think of this as putting out bait into areas where you know there are the kinds of fish you want to catch.

Once prospects are aware of and interested in your company's offerings, they may need more convincing to "take a bite" and take the next step in buying your product or service. They may need to get more information from your website, from your sales people, in your collateral material, from third party reviews, from information on various Internet sites or discussions groups, from other trusted people such as their friends, your customers, or perceived experts such as analysts and bloggers. (We'll talk about pull methods in Chapter 7.) While you can't control all of these channels directly, they can help to pull a prospect closer to making the decision to buy your products or services.

In conclusion, in its simplest form, marketing initiatives are needed to find out who, how, and why someone would buy the products or services being offered and help them to make the decision to purchase as quickly and easily as possible.

If you are ready, *let's do marketing!*

Great marketing comes from
insight, not guts.

Chapter 2:

A Marketing Inventory

Here is where the pedantic part kicks in because we need to honestly assess how much you already know about your business. For example, how much do you really know about your customers? Do you know what kind of people they are? Do you know where they get information? Do you know if they have budgets or the authority to spend them? Do you know how and where they shop? Do you know why they use or should use a product or service like yours?

These questions may seem too obvious. If they are, great – you are ahead of most others. If you don't know many of the answers, don't feel badly. This is more common than most people admit, yet these questions are the keys to unlocking the secrets of marketing.

In this chapter, we'll pose 30 such questions. While you shouldn't answer each one in detail now, take only one minute to think about each question and honestly consider if you really know the answer. If you do, move on to the next question. If you don't know the answer, highlight the question and then move on to the next question.

Do not worry about how much is or is not highlighted. This isn't a competition. It's an inventory of what you already have in your marketing war chest. We want to make sure that you are well equipped before making any marketing decisions or executing any marketing initiatives. This exercise will help us to make sure that we are going after the right targets with the right tools and the right messages.

**(I) No Time
30 MIN TO-DO**

My Marketing Inventory

You may have multiple answers for each question, such as different industries that you sell to or a variety of buyer ages. The more specific you can be, the better. Remember, don't take time to write each answer down now. Take just one minute for each question to think if you really know the answer and highlight those that you don't.

Section 1: Your Prospects & Customers

1a. Do you sell to other businesses (B to B) or to individual consumers (B to C)? If B to B, what size (revenue or # of employees) and type of companies (industry, public/private, domestic/international, franchised/wholly owned, for -profit or non-profit, etc.)?

1b. Who ultimately buys (approves the purchase of) your product or service? Can you describe that person in terms of: job title (including homemaker, student, unemployed), gender, age, income and education level, professional and personal interests?

1c. Who uses the product or service? Is it the same or different person(s) than the buyer? Can you describe the user(s) in terms of: job title, gender, age, professional and personal interests?

1d. Who participates in the purchase decision? Are there multiple people or a committee? If so, what role does each person play?

1e. What other types of people, companies, or industries would you like to sell to? Why?

Section 2: The Buying Process

2a. What steps do prospects go through when evaluating your products or services? Do they talk with people inside your company? Do they use your website or other marketing collateral?

2b. How long does it take for them to evaluate your product or service and make a yes or no decision?

2c. Do prospects utilize requests for proposals (RFPs) or do they require other formal methods of evaluation?

2d. Do prospects typically require references or other purchasing input before making a purchase decision? When in the buying cycle is this required?

2e. Do you need to have product demonstrations available during the buying process? Can the demos run on their own or must they be done by a company representative?

2f. Do prospects require a trial period when they can use the product or service risk free? Do they insist on a return policy or some other warranty in order to purchase your product or service?

2g. Is the product or service required to be part of the prospect's budgeting process or can it be purchased anytime?

2h. How often do you win deals? Why do you lose deals?

Section 3: Your Marketing Channels

3a. What magazines, websites, blogs, newsletters, TV, radio or other media are your prospects (users, influencers and buyers) reading or watching?

3b. Do they read or watch at work (during work time) or at home (on their own time)?

3c. What tradeshows do they attend?

3d. Which associations are they members of?

3e. Who are the industry analysts and other thought leaders in your market?

Section 4: Your Competition

4a. Who else sells a similar product or service?

4b. What other ways can someone accomplish the same thing that your product or service can do for them? Can they do it themselves manually or using other tools? Why is it better to use a product or service like the one you offer?

4c. Does your product or service replace another existing solution or must new budget money be allocated to acquire your product or service?

4d. What makes your product or service a better value to a prospect than the competitive offerings?

4e. What are your company and product or service weaknesses relative to the other solutions available?

4f. What can happen to prospects if they don't use your product or service? What risks do they expose themselves to if they don't buy your solutions?

4g. Are you priced competitively? Where does your pricing fall relative to your competitors'? What about your price relative to other means such as manual or substitute solutions from question 4b?

4h. Do you admire any of your competitors' products or services or their marketing techniques? If so, why?

Section 5: Your Market

5a. What are the key trends in your market today and over the next 3-5 years?

5b. Do you consider your market crowded or do you have one of the few offerings of its kind?

5c. What are your short- and long-term market share goals?

5d. What does your company want to be known for?

Congratulations!

You have completed the first major step in creating your marketing plan. Don't sweat it if the pages are all colored from your highlighting. In the next chapter, we'll talk about getting answers and filling in the missing pieces toward having total marketing intelligence.

Chapter 3:

Filling in the Blanks

Now that you've completed your marketing inventory, you now know what you don't know! The inventory was an important step because when you determine what types of marketing, positioning and messaging are needed, you will have the proper information to make the best possible decisions. Without every marketing inventory question answered, you are essentially *hoping* you shoot the right target with the right ammunition.

⊘ No Time
NO-NO

"Hope" is too risky for most businesses.

In order to minimize waste and frustration, our challenge now is to fill in the missing answers from our marketing inventory. To do this, I'll present you with research options for each section of the inventory that you just conducted:

Section 1. Your Prospects & Customers
Section 2. The Buying Process
Section 3. Your Marketing Channels
Section 4. Your Competition
Section 5. Your Market

I'll explain how you go about getting the missing information and the pros and cons of each approach. At the end of the explanations, there will be a *To-Do* for you to fill in. The *To-Do* asks you to choose what method you will use and a specific plan for getting that information filled in.

<u>Section 1: Your Prospects & Customers</u>
Refer to the Marketing Inventory questions 1 a – e

It is amazing to me as a marketing professional how much can be gained by a simple conversation, and yet how few business people themselves actively engage personally with their target customers. It's as easy as picking up the phone or going to the place where you know customers will be, such as a store, a tradeshow, or an association meeting. People, in general, are eager to share their opinions – especially as a customer to help a vendor that they have purchased from.

The best way to understand your customers and prospects is to interact with them directly. Simply talk to a few of them. Ask lots of questions and listen quietly. This can be accomplished in person (ideally) or over the phone. Some data can be obtained by sending email or questionnaires, but do this only for quantitative (objective) answers that you are seeking such as their age, their gender, or the specific magazines they read. However, for the more qualitative (subjective) questions that we considered in the marketing inventory in Chapter 2, it is far better to talk directly with your customers and prospects.

Consider setting up a customer advisory council to use as a regular sounding board for important issues. Advisory councils can meet in person, over the phone, or via online forums (or a combination of these methods). If you are facilitating the forum, have regular interaction and try to remain as objective as possible when presenting things to the group for their feedback. You can use

Actionize.com, LinkedIn, Yahoo, Google Groups or other free services to host private forums. Advisory councils provide invaluable feedback on products and services, marketing ideas and other subjective questions. Be sure that you have a good cross-section of your customer base and recognize when the group's opinions may be skewed by a strong leader or "group think" dynamics. If you are going to use group meetings, try to augment them with a few one-on-one conversations so that you can validate the overall information gathered.

Do you need to talk to hundreds of people? Not usually. It's hard to say how many will make the difference as that depends on the type of product or service that you offer. For example, a commodity product that is used by all types of people will need to have a greater variety of customers inputting their preferences and uses for the product. A product built specifically for a niche' market may not require as many customers since the targets may use and purchase the product similarly. However, never assume anything until you do the research and start to see patterns.

In much of my own consulting work, I usually see the patterns and exceptions emerge after 10-15 interviews. Other means to finding out about your customers and prospects include:

Type of research	Pros	Cons
Online surveys	• Inexpensive to administer. • Lots of tools available that are relative easy to use (e.g. SurveyMonkey, Zoomerang, Constant Contact, etc.). • Great for quantitative	• Impersonal so not good for qualitative questions. • Results will be better if questions are constructed by professionals who know the implications of asking

	data collection such as questions that are answered either yes or no or can be answered with a number or quantity.	things in certain ways. Depending on how the question is asked, it may unintentionally skew the answers.
	• Rapid response. Easy to analyze and see immediate results.	• You should use an opt-in list to invite survey participants.
	• People enjoy taking online surveys so response rates are good.	
Paper based surveys (administered in person or via post/mail)	• Familiar format for many people. • Good for quantitative data sought.	• Not as easy to administer as online (but will depend on your customers and ability to reach them electronically) • May require mailing to and from interviewee or individuals to administer onsite – both are costly. • Usually more expensive due to postage/paper. • Not as ecofriendly as online surveys. • Harder to analyze results and may take longer. • Need list of potential participants though opt-in is not necessarily required.

Telephone surveys	• Same benefits as paper based but often can be done more quickly. • If telemarketers use an online survey system to record data, you can analyze results immediately. • Can gather some qualitative information if interviewers are trained properly.	• If you need to hire people to collect and/or analyze data, it can be expensive. • Hard to reach certain types of people via phone in general and because people screen calls using caller ID. • Must use opt-in calling list and respect requests for opt-out. • Some people may be turned off by the intrusion without an invitation to call.
Internet research (e.g. keyword searches, blogs, reading discussion groups, etc.)	• Takes time but usually inexpensive. • If source is good such as a user blog or discussion group, this can be a great way to learn without disrupting your customers or competitors.	• Unless coming from the customer/prospect directly, not necessarily reliable so use information smartly. • The information you locate may not be particularly useful or on point. It may be wise to have a search engine expert help do efficient searches. For example, there are many smart tricks to using Google which can help tune your queries to get more focused results.
Internal databases of customer	• You may have some databases or lists of customer information—be sure to use them and use	• Small businesses often do not have such organized data nor per-

information	them carefully! You can enhance your existing list with info purchased from a data supplier (e.g. Axciom, Experian, etc.) to append demographic information and broaden your understanding of your customers. It won't tell you everything you need to know qualitatively but it can reveal new info about your customers.	sonnel trained to maintain such data. • Doing this isn't always easy and requires some technical ability. • Purchased demographic data can be expensive depending on quantity and type of data needed.
Internal Personnel (e.g. sales, support staff)	• Easy to access and inexpensive sources of "opinion" information.	• Opinions are cheap, but still can be helpful. Just use the subjective information wisely.
Third party analysts, thought leaders, and media (person-to-person or via articles and reports)	• Another good source of subjective but important opinion data, if they are willing to share their opinions without a fee. • By developing these relationships, mutual benefits can be gained from brainstorming ideas, sharing contacts, and co-creating opportunities.	• These people often require some fee to share their "expertise." Be wary of the free favors that may result in you owing them sooner than later. At minimum, their salespeople will hound you to become a paying client. • Understand how and where these third party experts are getting their information. You probably don't need more speculation, but rather real data.
Focus Groups	• Can help shed light on issues quickly and pro-	• Can be expensive. • Depending on type of

| (in-person or using an online focus group tool) | fessionally.

• Can be used for quantitative and qualitative data.

• May prove very insightful as third parties have less to risk by asking and hearing honest answers from customers and prospects.

• Can actually be used to educate a small group of prospects at the same time regarding the issue and solution available. | target participants, may be hard to recruit.

• Facilitator may not represent your product or service as well as you can.

• 'Group Think' and other group dynamics may cloud findings. |

⏱ **No Time**
15 MIN TO-DO

Your Customers and Prospects

Refer back to Chapter 2 and look at the Section 1 questions in the Marketing Inventory. For each question that you highlighted, note here how, who, and when will you get the answers.

Example: *For questions 1.c, 1.d, and 1.e: By June 30, I will interview Joe in the Sales group and thereafter 5 customers that Joe has sold to. I will ask Joe for introductions to these customers.*

_____

_____

_____

_____

_____

_____

_____

Section 2: The Buying Process
Refer to the Marketing Inventory questions 2a - h

Here too, talking directly with your customers is best. If it's at all possible, try to talk to prospects that have decided NOT to become your customers. Ask them why they decided not to purchase your product or service. Those inevitably are the richest sources of data about the buying cycle, competition and other marketing gems.

You should also talk to your sales people and other people involved with front line sales activities in your company. Their perspectives are important, but must be balanced with external customer validation as well. Sales people will never admit to their own shortcomings so you need to hear how and why customers bought and why others did not.

You can use surveys – online, telephone, paper-based – but the buying process is usually laden with exceptions and never the same from one company to the next. Hearing it from several sample customers is so valuable that I recommend not putting paper or telemarketers between you and the customers.

The Buying Process

Refer back to Chapter 2 and look at the Section 2 questions in the Marketing Inventory. For each question that you highlighted, make a note of how, who, and when you will get the answers.

Example: For questions 2e and 2f: I will also ask Mary in the Sales group about her thoughts on the buying process. I will include these questions in the interviews I do with the 5 customers (from Joe) noted previously.

<u>Section 3: Your Marketing Channels</u>
Refer to the Marketing Inventory questions 3a - e

Our challenge here is to identify the key places where your potential consumers look for trusted information about related products or services. Many times you can find low cost ways to have quality interaction and influence with target customers in industry or recreational forums, especially in the geographies that you want to operate in. We'll talk more in Chapter 7 about the types of things you can do such as write articles, do presentations, and other low-cost, high impact programs. For now, we want to continue filling in our marketing inventory with understanding the channels, or as I like to refer to them, the *customer watering holes*.

🕒 **No Time
15 MIN TO-DO**

Baseline Customer Watering Hole List

Build a starting list of watering holes that you know of. Think about the magazines, newspapers, online newsletters, websites and blogs you read or are aware of that contain information related to your products or services. Consider the professional events you have attended in the last few years and the ones you didn't attend but wish you had. Add to that list the associations you belong to or are aware of that relate to your product or service. Lastly, name any analysts or other thought leaders that you know are often quoted or publish information in your industry.

Magazines:

_____

_____

_____

Newspapers:

_____

_____

_____

Newsletters:

_____

_____

Blogs/Websites:

_____

_____

Tradeshows, conferences and other events:

_____

_____

Associations:

_____

_____

Analysts and other industry thought leaders:

_____

_____

_____

Next, send your draft list to other employees and/or colleagues asking them for any other additions they can think of.

⏲ No Time
5 MIN TO-DO

Get colleagues' input on baseline list

List the people you will send your draft list to get their additional ideas and input:

_____

_____

_____

Once you have this list of your own ideas and those of your colleagues, you are ready to add other ideas that your customers and prospects may contribute.

By now you know that I am going to once again suggest *talking to your customers and prospects*! If necessary, you can use more indirect means instead of face-to-face or telephone contact. An online survey, telemarketing survey, or even a simple email can be used to query target customers with the questions of what they read and what related events they attend.

✓ No Time
TIP

Whether you query your customers and prospects in person, on the phone, via email, or use a paper-based survey, be sure to first ask them an open-ended question such as, "What publications do you read?" Usually, this will reveal to you which ones they read regularly and astutely. You can then prompt them to identify others from a list of publications, events, associations, and conferences that you compiled beforehand from your own brainstorming and by asking colleagues. Survey as many people as you can and look for trends and anomalies. When you aren't seeing new data trends, then you know that you have enough data collected. The goal is to confirm that your list actually includes the top places prospects can be reached effectively. This list will help us determine where you should invest your marketing attention in terms of pitching articles, exhibiting, and doing other promotional activities. It will even help you focus on the places where you need to stay plugged-in and in the know.

Customer Watering Holes

Refer back to Chapter 2 and look at the Section 3 questions in the Marketing Inventory. For each question that you highlighted, note here how, who, and when will you get the answers.

Example: I will send an online survey to 20 customers. I will select these names from the customer database. The names will be selected by August 1 and the survey sent via email by August 2.

_____

_____

_____

_____

_____

_____

_____

<u>Section 4: Your Competition</u>
Refer to the Marketing Inventory questions 4a - h

> ## The best way to assess your competition is to be one of their customers.

It may not be practical or ethical to buy from your competitors but if it is possible, do it! You should compare the products and services themselves, but also you should evaluate the marketing, sales and support processes, and overall user experience. After all, the *entire offering* is what determines the outside perspective, so don't just open up the 'box' and examine what's inside. Look at the offering in terms of its packaging, its distribution channel, pricing, its support network and information. All of these things can be equally important differentiators.

If you can have a neutral third party consultant do the competitive comparison, even better. Have that third party become a customer of both your company and your competition's. Have the consultant provide honest comparative feedback on the entire experience. In this way, you don't impose your own biases and parental blindness on your own "perfect" offering.

You should also ask your customers and prospects who they believe to be your competition and if they have any opinions to share. As noted before, when talking to your customers and prospects, you can ask them in the form of a phone interview, survey, or email. The advisory council may be very helpful in sharing its knowledge about competitors. However, since they are already customers, they may be somewhat biased toward your offering simply because they are "part of your team."

Analyst reports, media articles, and other such secondary research can be helpful in understanding your competition, too, but they may require high access fees. If so, judge the source and value of the data and see if it makes sense to purchase available information. You can usually find industry analysts by using Internet search tools like Google, Yahoo, LexisNexis, Dogpile, etc. You might also look at your competitors' websites to review their press releases and the articles written about them that are posted.

Your Competition

Refer back to Chapter 2 and look at the Section 4 questions in the Marketing Inventory. For each question that you highlighted, note here how, who, and when will you get the answers.

Example: I will order my top three competitors' products by July 25. I will then note the experience from order to delivery and use. I will summarize my analysis by September 1.

_____

_____

_____

_____

Section 5: Your Market
Refer to the Marketing Inventory questions 5 a - d

This is the toughest section to fill in. The honest answer is that you need to stay well informed. Reading relevant publications, attending relevant events, and meeting thought leaders are all part of the game. Some ways to accelerate your learning is to spend time on the Internet reading articles, reports and blogs of respected individuals. Unfortunately, it is often hard to determine which are relevant and worth your time and resources. Luckily, the customer watering hole list you compiled should help guide you.

✓ No Time
TIP

A great tip is to set up Google Alerts with a handful of key-words relevant to your product and service. It's easy and free to do this, and you decide how often you want to receive news that matches your keywords. Use your competitors' names, your own company and product and service names, and other such keywords that may provide clues as to what is happening in the market. Once set up (it literally takes about 1 minute per keyword), Google Alerts will then automatically deliver an email to you with a link to the information that is newly posted on the Internet. It's a poor man's clipping service but it works really well to keep you abreast of what is happening.

✓ No Time
TIP

You may also want to sign up for compiled press release head-lines from most of the wiring services such as PRnews, Business-Wire, and so on. You can't access everything for free but you can at least see the headlines and then do additional research on the refer-enced company's website if you want more information. Some mar-kets even have their own wire services (e.g. CSRwire) or daily newsletter compilations that are in effect, indices of industry news. These are excellent ways to painlessly stay on top of news in your specific area.

Analyst reports can also be purchased but are often expensive. You may be able to get the gist of the trend and data through ab-stracts but to acquire the entire report, they are usually offered only to paid subscribers or a one-time fee. Carefully assess if the report is worthwhile before plunking down a lot of money. A lot of good information is out there for free on the Internet and can be very helpful. I will, however, be the first one to say there is also a lot of junk out there too. So my best advice is to consider only those reports from the respected thought leaders that you identified on your marketing channel from the inventory.

⊘ No Time
NO-NO

As for conferences and industry events, there will always be some that we cannot afford to attend as either an exhibitor or attendee. Before you register to go to any such event and commit your precious time and money, really think about what your objective is and how you can accomplish it. For example, are there specific people or companies you want to check out? Are there sessions that you want to go to or are you just going to get a general sense of industry trends and news? If you haven't had experience with that specific event, you may want to ask fellow industry associates if they've attended in the past and if they recommend the event. In many cases, you will attend events and find only by being there if you can accomplish your mission. In truth, there is no exact science that can be applied to figure out in advance if an event will generate leads or other benefits for your business. Much of lead generation success depends on your own preparation before, during, and after the actual event. We'll talk more about this in Chapter 6.

⊘ No Time
TIP

Meanwhile, here's a good tip for events that you cannot or do not want to attend. Review the agendas for industry events to see what's newsworthy by the type of session topics and the speakers that are participating. Since you won't be there in the sessions, you won't have the benefit of getting the actual information. However, just knowing the "what" and "who" that are being presented can be helpful. Think of this like reading the headlines of the newspaper so at least you are aware of the major topics of interest and competitive thrust that is under way. If you are interested in a particular session or want to meet a specific presenter, you can usually contact them directly and request copies of their presentations *after* the event. Many are happy to share because they put the information together for the purpose of sharing. You aren't asking that presenter to do anything more than email you the existing slides. You might also ask about the presenter's opinion of the event so you can see if it is worthwhile to participate in the future. Remember that requesting information after an event can be done for conferences that are not put on by an analyst firm whose business is *selling* that content.

My last bit of advice is to make time to stay in tune. I know how busy you are and how little time you have to read and do the things I just noted in terms of staying abreast of your market. Because it's so important, take five minutes now to think about when you can make the time so it fits in with your lifestyle. Perhaps during lunch, you can read or attend webinars. Find 15 minutes first thing in the morning or in the evening after hours. If you need to make an appointment in your calendar to do market research each week, do it. Schedule it in as a meeting and if you need to, go somewhere where the phones and other people can't interrupt you for that period of time. Perhaps treat yourself to a latte in Barnes and Noble where you can sit quietly and "meet" with your industry reading regularly – and yes, I believe you can write that off as a business expense on your taxes!

Personally, I like to have industry articles and reports in paper format so that they are portable. Note that I am very serious about recycling and if I am printing, I use FSC (Forest Stewardship Council) approved paper. I am also evaluating mobile electronic means and encourage you to do the same. Having my reading pile handy allows me to make use of time when I am eating lunch quietly, waiting in the doctor's office, getting my car's oil changed, or going somewhere where I know I may have a few moments to read. In most cases, it takes only a few minutes to scan through the articles, so even a brief wait can be productive. A stream of information is critical to keeping you up to date on what's happening in the outside world as well as imbibing you with new ideas and potential issues to contend with. I consider this required exercise for the business brain. It is important to the health of your business and to you as a successful business person. As one of the greatest marketing companies, Nike, reminds us: "Just Do It!™"

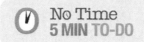

My Plan to Stay in Tune

My Google Search and Alert keywords include:

_____

_____

_____

_____

My regular reading list will include (may also include webinars and other informational media sources): *Hint: refer to the list of watering holes from the marketing inventory. These are the things that your prospects are learning from which means you should too!*

_____

_____

_____

I will make time to learn every:

_____ day _____week _____ month

Now set meetings up for yourself to do this right in your calendar:

The schedule for the next six months is:

_____

_____

_____

_____

_____

Congratulations! You now have a short-term marketing attack plan! You have the questions you need answered and how you are going to get those answers. Getting those answers may take some time, but you know that once you have them, planning out your tactical marketing plan gets a whole lot easier and smarter. In the next chapter we will build on what you just accomplished by creating and communicating your marketing message to your current and future customers.

In real estate, it's about location.
In marketing, it's about position.

Chapter 4:
Position with Precision

Your positioning statement is a concise set of words that clearly tell a prospective buyer who you are and why he or she should buy your product or service. This should ideally include why he or she needs or wants it and why yours is better than other solutions available. Sound easy? It's definitely not.

Companies can spend endless hours and significant money to nail down productive positioning. I am a proponent of having as perfect positioning as possible—but within reason. Not only does it help sell more products and services, but it's a real pain to go back and change your website, collateral, and other marketing assets that carry an old or inaccurate message. Plus, when your positioning is done well, everything else such as pricing, copy development, and all your design work is much easier to do and validate. For example, it's easy to get wowed by pretty graphics or interesting design concepts, so the positioning acts as a filter or scorecard that can be used to determine what a "good" representation of your business is, and what is not. Remember, while we do love creativity, its best when it is part of a business strategy. Your positioning provides that frame.

With the marketing inventory completed, you now have the ability to create a precise positioning statement.

A positioning statement basically says what you provide, why is it the best, who it benefits and how.

The positioning statement should be reflected in some form within all of your marketing work. Even if the words themselves change, the meaning should remain intact.

Here is a straightforward way to develop a positioning statement. Just fill in the blanks within these two sentences:

My Positioning Statement

*For [describe target customers/businesses:]*_____

[Your Company:] _____ provides

[Describe product/service in layman terms:] _____

_____

_____that

*[The benefit of using your product/service instead of alternative means to address the problem:]:*_____

_____

_____.

Unlike other solutions, our product *[compared to the competition, describe why your offering is uniquely valuable:]*

_____

_____.

The key to this positioning statement is making it concise and easy to understand. This becomes your "elevator pitch" that you can use to introduce yourself at a cocktail party or to your fellow fans during halftime at a ballgame, or on your LinkedIn, Facebook and MySpace professional profiles. With this statement in hand, you can quickly validate the information in your brochures, website, and other materials to make sure they properly reflect what your company offers and why.

No Time TIP

While we'll discuss testing the entire marketing plan later in Chapter 8, don't wait to test your positioning. Do it as soon as possible with people that you know well and tell them to be brutally honest. Ask your mom, your neighbor, and other people who know nothing about your business. Ask your company colleagues and customers. After he or she reads it or hears it from you orally, ask them to paraphrase it back to see if they understood the meaning. Don't assume they are stupid if they don't get it! Probe to figure out what you didn't communicate well. Sometimes it's a simple word change. Sometimes you incorrectly assume that your audience already has knowledge and experience in the area. Testing the positioning, even informally, is a great way to get other brains to contribute by giving them something short to critique. It's also a great relationship building tool too as you are indirectly complimenting your "advisors" and giving them a stake in your business. You may be surprised by who ends up being your best evangelists! Take advantage of this free opportunity.

Marketing Messaging

Marketing messages are essentially the words that help you to you convey the positioning. While we can spend a ton of time explaining and doing messaging, we will (as expected!), cut to the chase.

Your message must include your positioning and convey the image you want people to take away when exposed to it. So, do you want to be the safe car or the luxury vehicle? Are you Dunkin Donuts® or Starbucks®? Messaging supports your brand and how you reflect it in your marketing materials, pricing, programs, and overall outward facing company interactions. Positioning and messaing are also critical to your internal communications and operations to help them prioritize and act according to the desired company image and focus!

My Company Image

The following are three quick and simple exercises to help cull out the image and reputation that you want for your company. Your messaging will communicate your brand and key sales information out to potential customers, investors and other critical targets.

1. List the words that you want people to use when describing your company: *(e.g. innovative, inexpensive, quality, smart, organized, etc.)*

_____

_____

_____

_____

_____

2. If you could pick any celebrity (alive or dead, real or fictional, Hollywood, literary, political – essentially, someone well known to the public) to be your company spokesperson, who would it be and why? Describe the qualities that make them ideal to hypothetically represent your product or service.

_____

_____

_____

3. What other companies (in any industry) do you feel have the same or similar attitude or look and feel as yours or that you would like to be more like? Why?

_____

_____

_____

_____

No Time
30 MIN TO-DO

My Company Message

Answer the following questions as succinctly and accurately as possible. Be sure that for each answer, you can back the claim up with real, measurable information.

1. What is the problem your company solves and for who?

_____

_____

2. Why is your solution unique and a good value to the target buyers?

_____

_____

_____

3. What will someone gain if they use your product or service?

_____

_____

_____

4. What can happen if someone doesn't use your product or service?

_____

_____

_____

This type of information can be very helpful to designers, copywriters, and others who will take the positioning and messaging to create artwork, logos, collaterals and such for you. When you receive things to review or are creating them yourself, you can review the positioning statement and the messaging concepts to make sure that the resulting marketing work is aligned.

Pricing is both an art and science.
implying both cost and value.

Chapter 5:
Practical Pricing

While entire books are devoted to pricing theory and methodologies, in this book we will boil down the essential information you need to effectively price your product or service. Please note that there may be important aspects of pricing that apply to your *specific* offering that we cannot cover in this intentionally short overview. For example, with software, there are many types of pricing models, e.g., named and concurrent users, onsite hosted versus online leased use (also known as Software as a Service (SaaS)). You may have customer financing considerations, such as in the automotive industry, or metered use as in the energy sectors. Please utilize this chapter as a starting point to think about new pricing or as part of your due diligence process to validate existing pricing.

Pricing can help position your product or service and as such is a strategic decision as well as a practical one. Pricing inevitably defines your customer base, competition and ultimately your profits.

The 4 C's of PriCCCCing

There are the legendary 4 Ps of marketing that we mentioned briefly in Chapter 1: Product, Price, Promotion, and Place. There are also, the infamous, 4 C's of pricing: Cost, Competition, Customers and Change.

Cost

The simplest variable to determine should be your cost. You need to calculate the expenses accumulated when developing, delivering, marketing, selling, and supporting a product or service. Be sure to include less obvious factors such as royalties, shipping, and insurance. In the end, you want to know what the *per unit* (product) or *per delivery* (service) cost is. This usually depends on your volume, so for simplicity's sake, utilize your current volume or your short term anticipated volume to know what the worst case expense per unit will be. As your business grows and gains economies of scale, you can adjust your pricing, or, ideally, enjoy higher margins!

Your per unit cost is your baseline to apply the desired margin. In some industries, there is a standard margin range expected. More likely, your competition and customers' tolerance will set the price that then subsequently determines your margin. By knowing what the cost per unit or per delivery is, you will at least know "how low you can go" with your price and margin. In the worst scenario, you may find that your costs are higher than the target price. This is not a happy revelation but it is far better to find out *early* and figure out what to do, than lose money on every deal just to remain competitive. I know this may seem rather silly, but I see this happen with too many businesses!

No Time
30 MIN TO-DO

My Cost Per Unit

If you don't already know what your cost per unit or per delivery is, you can use the following as a rough estimate. Be as specific as possible and calculate each cost. Use "Not Applicable (N.A.)" for costs that do not apply to your business. You can use total cost and divide by the estimated units to be sold. If you use a program like QuickBooks, you can pull the per unit cost right from there, or if still not sure, ask your accountant.

Product Development
(include people, tools, systems, etc.)   _____
Packaging   _____
Manufacturing   _____
Product Support   _____
Administrative Support
(people)   _____
Administrative Support
 (supplies & office equipment)   _____
Royalties   _____
Commissions   _____
Cost of Sales   _____
Installation   _____
Service Delivery
 (gas, tools, vehicle leases, etc.)   _____
Legal Fees
(contract review, trademarks,
patents, insurance, etc)   _____
Office Space/Rent   _____
Office Utilities
 (e.g. phone service, Internet service,
 electricity, gas/oil, water, etc.)   _____
Existing marketing
 (e.g. website hosting, brochures, etc.)   _____
Other: (specify)

_____   _____

Total Cost: _____

Number of Units forecasted: _____

Per Unit Cost: _____

Competition

The next step is to compare your price with prices of your competitors. Hopefully your previous competitive analysis in the marketing inventory provided some data, but you will probably need to do some deeper investigation. Try to assess, apples-to-apples, what the competition charges for the same product or service in the same sales circumstances. Don't compare a standalone product or service with the same component bundled into a larger package. For example, if you sell a product that requires installation service, a bundled package may significantly change the pricing. Also factor in discounting practices and overall lifetime cost of ownership and maintenance costs required by your customers to continue using the product or service.

Depending on where you want to position your offering, you might want to be higher or lower than your competitors. Review Chapter 4 and your positioning. Do you want your product to be perceived as the Cadillac or the Kia? Think about your desired and perceived position in the marketplace and try to find the price that will position you where you want to be.

(I) No Time
30 MIN TO-DO

Competitive Pricing Analysis

Competitor	**Price**
(list highest to lowest and include your own offering in the list!)	
1. _____	_____
2. _____	_____
3. _____	_____
4. _____	_____
5. _____	_____
6. _____	_____

Customers

The same products or services offered by different companies may be priced completely differently. One vendor may "get away" with charging higher prices simply because there is a perceived added value from that particular vendor. That premium demonstrates the power of branding. People will pay the extra money feeling that the brand name is reputable and that the company will stand behind the product and/or service. Sometimes a brand simply represents cache' or it is perceived to be cool. Therefore, people may want that specific brand even when there are higher quality, lower cost options. Consider all the brands out there with premium pricing while many markets also support cheaper, generic ("no name") offerings that are otherwise identical.

Other reasons why some companies can charge premium prices include the availability of complementary products and services or superior support. Remember that a product is indeed more than "what's in the box," and customers are willing to pay more to be sure they will be successful using the product. Consider the price of an Apple® MAC versus most Microsoft® Windows PCs as a case in point. Apple computers were originally designed to be easier to use for non-technical individuals. Though they deliver the same end result (computer services), the systems have always commanded a higher price which reflected this value to the company's target markets. Now with the additional "value" of being more attractive, cool, and reliable, Apple continues to enjoy higher pricing for their systems across a very broad market.

In some industries, there are ways to calculate the amount that a customer will pay for your product or service by estimating your share of their overall planned budget. Sometimes this percentage can be derived from analyst reports that forecast spending on specific products and services. Otherwise, you can also ask your customers for that data if you really want to go down this often complicated path.

As you well know by now, your customers and prospects are

the most valuable sources that can provide insight into the price elasticity of your product or service. Informally, you can ask them how much they think the product or service is worth.

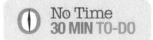

Elasticity Analysis

If you haven't already, ask customers the following questions:

1. Does the product or service increase their productivity or reduce employee costs? Can your customer quantify this?

_____

_____

_____

_____

_____

_____

2. Did he/she feel they got a fair deal and acceptable value from the product or service? If not, why?

_____

_____

_____

_____

3. Did the price help or hurt their ability to make a purchase decision quickly?

_____

_____

_____

Change

Pricing is not a static, one-time event. Market prices should be continually monitored and, if necessary, your pricing structure will need to change to accommodate market changes. There simply isn't any such a thing as "the right price." In the end, it boils down to "the price is the best possible one for now."

Setting prices can involve sophisticated scientific processes and analyses, but in reality, pricing almost always relies on subjective judgment. Using the four C's can help guide your judgment and allow you to choose an appropriate price.

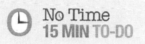

No Time
15 MIN TO-DO

Pricing Summary

My per unit cost: _____

My customer's recommended price _____

The highest price competition _____

The lowest price competition _____

My price _____

My margin _____

Quality, not quantity,
is what matters.

Chapter 6:
Acquiring Leads

In the Marketing Inventory, we used Section 3 to help identify the key watering holes where your prospects and customers get their related information. Now, we need to plan your marketing placement. This is where and how you will put your messages about your product or service in places such as advertisements, websites, magazine articles, tradeshows, and so on.

In Chapter 2, we talked about *push* versus *pull* marketing. As a quick review, push marketing means proactively getting in front of your qualified prospects to let them know about your product, service, or company even if they are not looking for such a solution. You can think of push marketing in terms of acquiring new leads. Pull marketing is, once you get prospects' attention, how you move them along the buying process to purchase your product or service quickly and efficiently.

In this chapter, we focus on push marketing techniques. In the next chapter, we'll turn our attention to pull marketing.

There are thousands of places to "push" your message. Because of cost, many opportunities are impractical for the majority of businesses. For example, unless we see another dot.com pre-bubble Venture Capital (VC)-sponsored environment, I don't expect to see too many small businesses advertising nationally during the Superbowl or World Cup. However, depending on your market and specific offering, local cable TV may offer some fantastic opportunities. We'll explore a number of ways to get your message out, but remember that we could never cover all channels that are available. Therefore, I will provide you with filters that you can apply to any marketing opportunity.

Filter #1: Consider the Audience. Unless the marketing opportunity clearly gets you in front of your specific target customers, don't be tempted by "reach" or other quantitative potential. It's sexy but not very smart to reach lots of people with an irrelevant message that ultimately wastes your time and money. I often hear of businesses sinking all of their available marketing resources into PR and trying to get on Oprah, People Magazine, The Today Show, and other national media. Not only are those chances slim, but in fact may not change your business at all. You'll obtain major bragging rights for sure, but more business? Maybe. Before investing in any kind of marketing initiative, demand to know how many specific audience types the medium reaches, who they are, and what other similar companies have used each channel. This is important for filter #2.

Filter #2: Seek References. When evaluating a media or other marketing placement, ask for two or three references and call them to find out what worked or didn't work for them. You must assume that any references provided to you will have positive things to say simply because they are prescreened to say good things. Take advantage of this opportunity to talk to the person who used the medium and really question the return they received.

You should also inquire about how easy it was for them to work with the channel so that you understand your business investment beyond the dollars spent, e.g., your time and aggravation.

Filter #3: Assess the Cost. You can't always compare the cost of one program to all others out there to find the ultimate opportunity.

So here is a basic concept to evaluate your cost versus the price of your offering. For example, if your product or service is $100 and the cost of the program is $1,000, you need 10 successful sales just to break even. This is not so much a magic formula but good common sense. If you have done a similar marketing program and remember how many successful leads and sales you generated, then, of course, use that data. If not, be as conservative as possible. For example, maybe in the worst case scenario, can you justify the cost of the new program if you only close one deal? No doubt with marketing, there is always some trial and error. The only thing you can do is to minimize your errors by minimizing your investment in risky marketing propositions.

⊘ **No Time**
NO-NO

Sure, big risks can mean big rewards, but in small businesses, *big marketing risks can also mean big bankruptcies.* So now let's turn our attention to some tried and true ways that can help generate leads.

Finding Prospects

Remember, there are two ways to push information out:
1. Sending information specifically to a list of prospects.
2. Putting your message in places where prospects may see it.

Lead Lists

You can buy lists of prospect names from various places including list brokers, list vendors, and so on. Industry associations, publications, and other places that have members or subscribers usually also sell their membership lists. Even tradeshows and websites sell their lists.

⊘ **No Time**
NO-NO

Beware. There are many bad lists out there and the data may come from multiple sources. Some companies aggregate data so that the records have multiple fields of demographic and other information beyond the prospects' contact information. List providers may even segment their lists further by creating affinity groupings so that they can sell lists of people "most likely to buy" a specific type of product or service.

The cost of lists varies greatly depending on the volume of names and types of data that you are interested in. Email addresses, for example, are typically more expensive than postal addresses.

✓ **No Time**
TIP

If you decide to purchase names from any source, be sure to get some sample records and test them. You can ask for other customer references and start with a small list to try it before you commit to the whole list. Also make sure that your vendor abides by the latest opt-in laws and ask how the vendor actually obtains the data.

Be sure to ask for the specific parameters you want in your leads such as age, income levels, job titles, etc. – all the things you identified in your marketing inventory. Depending on the list provider, you may be able to purchase only the data fields that you want. Some list providers only offer data based on predefined packages so you may end up with more data than you really need. Once you obtain a list, you can further segment it to deliver the most relevant information to the specific people. You'll use the list of marketing lead generation programs described later in this chapter to decide what you want to send to your list of prospects.

The other way to get prospect names is to "show up" in the venues that potential customers patronize. Specifically, places like the tradeshows, magazines, webinars and websites that we identified in the marketing inventory (Section 3). These are the places where your customers said that they learn about similar new products or services – we called them the "customer watering holes." While there are any number of watering holes available, consult your inventory list for the popular ones that give you the best chance of putting your message in front of your prospects.

Push Marketing/Lead Generation Methods

With an expanding list of marketing techniques, programs, and initiatives available, let me present you some of the most common ways to attract new leads. It is helpful to think about each type of opportunity and consider which ones make sense for your business

Is there a magical mix of what types of programs and how many should be used? Unfortunately, no. The forthcoming list lead generation programs can be used to consider ways that may or may not make sense for your specific business. However, in addition to common sense, the decision about what to do and how much to do often depends on trial and error to see firsthand what actually works for your business and your specific prospects.

Below in the list of marketing ideas, I raise important issues to consider before embarking on that specific type of marketing initiative. Keep in mind that even when you have clear ROI comparisons between initiatives, you always want to manage a balance of honing existing programs and trying new ones. *Your goal is to generate the highest quality leads at the least cost.* The only practical way to do this in a small business is to carefully plan, measure, and evaluate each marketing program before, during, and after implementation.

Marketing experience can help in these judgments, but because markets and technology changes so fast today, the best marketers strive to keep themselves and their programs fresh. So, while I will present you with the most common types of marketing programs, don't be shy in applying creativity and innovation to the methods. The only rule is to diligently build in some measurement criteria that will help you to determine success or failure. Measurements can be as simple as number of leads generated or amount of business closed. They may be harder to measure metrics such as increased customer satisfaction or brand recognition. You might even have measurement goals around cost/lead or reduction in sales cycle. Select the measurements that you can measure easily but also that will directly impact your business. For smaller businesses, this usually means number of leads generated.

Advertising

I am using the term "advertising" to generically represent opportunities to place your message in front of people in some venue where they *may* see it. Unlike some other methods, advertising does not guarantee that a prospect will see, understand, act or otherwise "consume" the information. It's typically a passive method that hopes to present the right information to the right person, even if that person isn't specifically looking for it. Advertising usually involves a payment or barter arrangement. Depending on the venue, you may have to provide some or all of the artwork and finished ad.

Examples of advertising opportunities include:
- TV (national, local cable, Internet based, direct TV, infomercials)
- Radio (national, local, Internet, satellite)
- Magazine/newspaper (national, regional, local, Internet-based)
- Billboards (free standing, public transportation stations, trains, and buses, elevators, malls, etc. May be conveyed through paper or electronic means.)
- Phone books (regional, local, Internet-based)
- Internet and mobile phone ads (banners, affiliate listings, Google Adwords, web video ads, etc.)
- Flyers or other hardcopy information (handed out, placed at various stores or stations, etc.)
- Miscellaneous placement such as airplane banners, blimps, trucks, sandwich boards, on floors, etc.
- Sponsorships (social or cultural events, holiday parades, sport-

ing teams, public venues such as stadiums, fields, charity events, etc.)

Issues to consider: Make sure that you know the audience demographics and match them to your target prospects. You can't usually control who is exposed to the message and you'll inevitably pay for people viewing your ads that are not good prospects. You can't even ensure that a good target sees the ad, so be smart about how many potential eyeballs will really see your ad and how many you can actually influence. Advertising is often expensive and hard to measure precisely. Consider how you will know if the campaign is successful or not. Most advertising rates will quote some sense of how many people will be exposed to the ad. Common metrics are Cost per Thousand (CPM) or Cost per Million (CPMM) which signify how many people may see the ad (known as the impression). This is really a measurement of how many people read or subscribe to that media. It doesn't guarantee that many people will see it, will read it, or will remember your ad.

Only be impressed if there is tracking of who does read and remember the ads and if those eyeballs are literally in the heads of your potential buyers. With Internet advertising, usually the number of people who actually click on the ad to find out more information or to order can be measured. Reader response cards or surveys are still used to try to measure print advertising impact and effect. It is still tricky to determine an absolute success measurement with advertising, but when it is carefully planned and executed it can be a good means to exposing your message and building your brand.

Direct Mail

Direct mail is typically sending something physical such as a postcard, letter, or promotional item sent via old fashioned postal mail.

Two examples of types of direct mail opportunities include:
- Your own that you create and send
- Someone else's where your material is included (e.g. coupon mailers or envelope stuffers)

Issues to consider: You or the third party sender will need to obtain a mailing list (preferably opt-in which means people have signed up on their own to be on it). You may already have one from your own collection efforts or one can be acquired from a list broker or list vendor as was discussed before. Direct mail includes the cost of the list, the cost of creating the mailer (design and printing), plus the postage. All of this together can be expensive. This type of marketing is still quite common and generates on average a 1-3% return. This means that 1-3% of the recipients actually do act and purchase the product or service being offered. When focused on a targeted geography or demographic with personalized messaging, success rates can be higher.

Internet Email/Newsletters

Whether it's a fancy, professionally designed newsletter or a simple, text email, the Internet offers an inexpensive way to send information to prospects. The downside of this low cost opportunity is that many people take advantage of it and there is a proliferation of SPAM and email traffic overall. Subsequently, many people ignore or don't even receive many of the commercial emails sent to them because of the filters now set up to prevent mass emails from ever arriving into the recipients' inbox. Even newsletters and other electronic communications that people have signed up to receive are often subject to low view rates.

Example of Internet/Newsletter opportunities include:
- Your own
- Someone else's where your ad or materials are included

Issues to consider: First you will need an opt-in mailing list that includes email addresses. If you don't already have a list, you can purchase one, but again, this can be costly. Typically, email addresses are the trickiest part of a mailing list because of the strict regulatory laws and the ability for users to submit fake or inactive accounts. Internet mailings can be in the form of simple text emails, fancy newsletters or other HTML-based documents. Depending on what you want to create, there may be a cost to the design and implementation of the document.

The good news is that there are some really easy to use, low cost email campaign tools available via the Internet. There is usually a fee to use the tools, but there is no cost in sending out one or multiple email campaigns. Ideally, you want a way to capture the open and click rates as well as bad email addresses, and people's requests to unsubscribe. The email campaign tools should accomplish these tasks to help ensure that you are following CANN/SPAM regulations and that you do not offend your targeted prospects.

Media/PR

Doing effective public relations (PR) is both an art and a science. Reaching out to editors, journalists, bloggers, producers, and thought leaders is all part of PR. The goal is to get your company or offering covered by appropriate magazines, newspapers, websites, TV, radio, and blogs that your prospects may see and be influenced by. While helpful to have "third party" PR endorsements, you usually can't control the message or timing of the information put out.

Examples of media PR opportunities include:
- Articles or other content that you've created (proactive PR)
- Interviews where you are an expert or referenced in someone else's article or show (reactive PR)

Things to consider: PR can take both time and money to be successful. Depending on your target media, you may be able to offer relevant thought leadership material as a writer or inter-viewee. Hiring a PR consultant can be costly but may be very worthwhile if you cannot afford your own time or don't have the experience to pitch appropriately to the media. Some PR consultants will even work on a pay-for-placement basis which means you only pay them if they successfully place an article. The typical disadvan-tage of pay-for-placement is that you usually don't have any control about where your information will be placed.

Ø **No Time**
NO-NO

Keep in mind that PR typically "only" helps build awareness unless it can be tied to a call for action such as call or click to get more information. Incentives such as trials, giveaways or discounts are often used in conjunction with advertising and PR. Also keep in mind that PR is usually a long process. Monthly publications often plan four or more months in advance, so it may take time for your article to be accepted and then time for it to appear in the publica-tion. Successful PR utilizes repetitive pitching to targeted media. The more specific you can target your information to an outlet, the better.

✓ **No Time**
TIP

Remember to ask yourself, "Why should this editor or writer want to write about this?"

Tradeshows, Conferences and Association Meetings

Most of the time, tradeshows, conferences, and association meetings are face-to-face events and can have great benefits for small businesses by allowing valuable face-to-face contact with prospects. They can provide networking opportunities for leads and partnerships.

Examples of professional event opportunities include:

- A booth or other onsite venue to provide product and service information
- A presentation or keynote speech
- A hospitality room or place where you can entertain and meet with prospects
- A pre-event mailer to invite prospects to your booth, hospitality suite, or presentation.
- A post-event mailer or email to follow up with prospects that you meet at the event (or perhaps didn't).
- A game, entertainment or logo'ed giveaway (like logo shirts, keyring flashlights, pens, etc.) to attract people to stop by your booth to have fun while learning about your products and services. You can also include this information in a pre-mailer.
- Special pricing deals for your products and services when ordered during the event. You can advertise this in a pre-mailer.
- Collect business cards for a raffle of prizes or left over samples on the last day of the event.

Issues to consider: It is important to be selective about which tradeshows, conferences, and association meetings you choose to participate in as an attendee, vendor, or sponsor. With so many to choose from and each one typically requiring a large investment in time and money, be sure to use the filters presented at the beginning of the chapter to help you decide which, if any, events or memberships you want to add to your marketing plan.

Consider whether you want to reach a local, national, or international audience. Be sure that you understand the attendee demographics and their needs in order to get them to stop and talk to you. Once you determine the events that you will attend, be sure to think through what you can do before, during, and after the events to optimize your investment. For example, should you do a pre-show mailer to let people know you will be at the show? How about a post-show thank you email providing information that is tailored to each prospect?

When calculating the cost of an event, include booth fees, set-up and implementation fees (such as electrical and cleaning), travel expenses, marketing materials, and entertainment expenses. If you don't already own a booth and all the parts such as chairs, collateral holders, projection and computing equipment, etc., be sure to include the rental costs when calculating your overall event expenses.

Also consider the cost of the time lost by you and your staff by being at the event rather than minding the business back home.

Face-to-Face Seminars

Events unto themselves, face-to-face seminars also offer a great way to get in front of prospects.

Examples of face-to-face seminar opportunities include:
- Your own
- Participation in someone else's

<u>Issues to consider</u>: In arranging a seminar, you need a number of ingredients: a speaker, a topic of interest to your target prospects, a venue, a list of invitees, and possibly refreshments, equipment, invitations, and so on. Running a quality face-to-face seminar can cost money and, unfortunately, in this busy business world, getting people to leave their offices or homes to attend an offsite seminar requires as much luck as it does good planning.

You might consider charging for the seminar to recoup some or all of the cost. Prepaid registrations actually help ensure that your registrants have an incentive to actually show up. Oftentimes, people will sign up for free events but not show at the last moment because of conflicts, laziness, or other reasons. By charging for the event, you may get fewer registrants but typically those that pay prior are more committed to coming. For all face-to-face seminars, especially fee-based ones, you should offer a take-home element of the session such as a workbook, gift and/or other item that provides value to the attendee after the event itself. You can note this take-home gift in the marketing for the event as another good reason for prospects to attend. But don't forget that the most important reason people will attend any business event is to get the information or contacts that will benefit them personally at home or at work.

Webinars and Teleseminars

Teleseminars, via telephone conference calls, provide an audio-only experience unless you provide your participants with handouts to refer to while you are talking. Webinars are presentations given via the Internet, providing both audio and visual information. Most also include interaction with your audience through question and answer segments and sometimes real-time surveys. Participants log on to see your slides and video clips that you control while you present. Most webinars also allow participants to download a copy of the presentation materials. Webinar audio is provided via a call-in phone number or via the Internet. Both teleseminars and webinars are typically inexpensive to run and can provide good tracking of who registered and who attended. They can also be recorded to allow for future reference by attendees or those unable to attend the live event. Recorded files are great content for your website and can provide excellent support to optimize your search engine relevance.

Examples of webinar and teleseminar opportunities include:
- Your own one-time, webinar or teleseminar – delivered in real time and recorded for future viewing
- Recurring webinars or teleseminars – may be live or recorded
- Participation in someone else's webinar/teleseminar

<u>Issues to consider</u>: Webinars can be inexpensive to set up but keep in mind that you have little control over the participation of your audience. Although they may be connected physically, they may not be really tuned in to your presentation. However, depending on your presentation and audience, webinars can be effective to inform and educate prospects. Be sure to consider if your target audience can connect to a webinar easily and in an appropriate setting.

If participants work in a crowded office environment, you should offer the audio portion of the webinar via telephone rather than Internet audio requiring desktop speakers or headsets.

Telemarketing

Telemarketing is calling prospects to promote the product or service, a related event, or sales offer. You can use internal personnel to serve as telemarketers (sometimes called inside sales or telesales) or you can hire outside resources.

Examples of telemarketing opportunities include:
- Promote an upcoming event or special offer
- Try to interest prospects in your offering via a cold call or follow up call

<u>Issues to consider</u>: The cost to hire telemarketers may be prohibitive for many small businesses.

A list with phone numbers must be available that is legally in line with the latest federal and state regulations. Caller ID and the current trend of replacing land lines with cell phones make it difficult to reach target consumers, as does the overabundance of re-corded mass messages now going out to censoring prospects. Tele-marketing is often used in conjunction with other channels such as email. For example, you might call to follow up on an offer or event presented to prospects in the email. Even if your telemarketers only leave voicemail as a follow up, at least you are trying to get the prospects' attention using more than one method, in this case, both email and voicemail.

Search Engine Optimization (SEO)

SEO is a hot topic for marketers given its complexity and new-ness. It is the science behind having your website (or other web presence such as a blog or wiki) found easily by people looking for related information. In a nutshell, SEO is about having your web information properly organized and coded so that search engines like Yahoo and Google can index the information and ideally place it high up on the search results page. Further, SEO may involve buying keywords and taking advantage of search engine prefer-ences such as inbound links to your site and providing ongoing fresh content.

Example of SEO opportunities include:
- Ensuring that your existing web information is optimized for search results
- Looking into buying relevant keywords on search engines
- Maintaining fresh and relevant content on your site
- Asking other site webmasters and bloggers to link to yours

Issues to consider: If your product or service is one that con-sumers will typically search for on the Internet, SEO can be helpful to present your offering higher up on their search result lists. How-ever, if the type of solution like yours is unknown to the prospect, SEO may be a little tricky. You'll need to think about the type of words prospects would use to find a solution.

**✓ No Time
TIP**

You should always consider keywords describing the symptoms of the problem or other relevant word associations.

Frequent Buyer and Customer Loyalty Programs

Frequent buyer and customer loyalty programs are ways to get existing customers to buy more. The programs may be in the form of point accumulation and reward redemption, special discounts only available to existing customers, special member-only invitations, events and announcements, and so on.

Examples of frequent buyer and customer loyalty program opportunities include:
- Your own frequent buyer or loyalty program
- You can offer your products or services as rewards for other people's frequent buyer programs

Issues to consider: Member programs require two key pieces for success. First, they must be well communicated to the target participants. Second, they must be managed so that they are productively executed.

**⊘ No Time
NO-NO**

Be sure to check with your target participants on what is considered a good reward as some may not be able to accept cash or gifts. Consider alternative rewards such as future purchase discounts or charitable donations in that person's or company's behalf.

Because expectations may be high from similar programs in the consumer market, your loyalty program must be devised carefully and well managed so that you don't upset an otherwise happy and profitable customer. There are third party companies who will set up and manage programs for you, but be sure you feel confident that the company will treat your valued customers well and can best represent your company in terms of service, spirit, and organization. Also realize that loyalty programs, once initiated, must continue for quite some time until the accumulated rewards are used – they aren't something you can turn on or off easily.

Referral Programs

A referral program is a great way to get existing customers to help you acquire new leads. Because your customers are already knowledgeable about your products and services, referral programs should provide you with well-qualified leads. In addition, the original customer can benefit from helping another buyer, justifying his or her original purchase or receiving some specific reward from you.

Examples of referral program opportunities include:
- Your own referral program
- Participation in someone else's referral program

<u>Issues to consider</u>: Similar to frequent buyer and loyalty programs, referral programs must be carefully set up with clear terms and rules. They then must be well tracked and rewards must be properly delivered.

No Time™ Tricks of the Marketing Trade

In order to optimize your investment in any of the above programs, here are some means marketers commonly use:
- *Utilize an incentive* in each promotion, such as: "call now and get 2 free"...or "stop in our booth to get a free trinket"....or "the first 20 to register get a free book"...or "fill in this form and get a free download of a whitepaper." Rrequire the prospect to enter valid information before you provide the prize so that will have the

necessary information to qualify the lead.

- *Ensure you have a call to action.* This means tell the prospect what you want them to do after attending or viewing your program. Calls to action are typically: call, email, click, download, or other such "do now" commands to the prospect.
- *Use multiple forms of outreach.* If your marketing inventory says your targets use email and you send them invitations to seminars, never assume that is enough to get their attention. Consider using telephone follow-up calls to make sure they got the invitation or even remind them a day or two prior to the event so they are more likely to attend.
- *Utilize tests wherever possible.* Don't launch a multi-city seminar series until you do one and see how effective it is and can refine it to optimize its impact. Test a seminar topic or invitation with some prospects to see if it appeals to them before going further.
- *Quality is always better than quantity.* More seminars don't necessarily mean better prospects or even more prospects. Do things right and expand as you get the recipe for success that fits your specific business and timing.
- *Always follow up.* You want to reach the best possible prospects to attend your event, but also you must follow up with them after the event. What a waste it would be to run a great event and then not follow up with the leads to close deals. We'll discuss how and when to do this in the next chapter. It is worth repeating that you should never embark on a lead generation program unless you have the capacity and plan to do follow-up.

No Time
30 MIN TO-DO

Placing My Message

First, note the targeted media channels identified in your marketing inventory and then note how you will place your message there:

Targeted Watering Holes	How I Will Place My Message There	How I Will Measure Success
Example: MyTown Chamber of Commerce	*Contact president and offer to do a presentation at a future meeting*	*>10 qualified leads generated and >2 sales closed*

Now that we've discussed reaching out to prospects via push marketing techniques, let's move on to Chapter 7 where we'll talk about how to pull them in once you have obtained their interest.

Move leads into buying customers by helping
them make an informed, confident decision.

Chapter 7:
Fostering Leads

Once you have prospects interested in your product or service, they may not yet be convinced to buy. Maybe they need more information about what the product or service does. Maybe they need to better justify the cost versus the benefit. Maybe they need to figure out how to replace an existing product or service with yours, or to figure out how to finance the transaction. The first step in figuring out your *pull* marketing strategy is to, once again, revisit your marketing inventory. Take a look at the information covering the buying cycle.

In Section 2 of the Marketing Inventory, in the Buying Process, you should have uncovered what steps and information are needed for your prospects to move along the purchasing process.

There are some typical things that marketers do to provide prospects with information. The specific methods and tactics will vary depending on the product or service and from marketer to marketer. To start, here is a list of helpful ideas.

Lead Fostering Programs

First, anything that was on the lead acquisition/push marketing list in Chapter 6 is fair game to use as a lead fostering/pull method as well. This includes: advertising, direct mail, email, newsletters, PR, press releases, tradeshows, conferences, association meetings, in-person seminars, webinars, teleconferences, telemarketing and

SEO. While not all lead generation programs will be applicable to lead fostering, you should at least consider including existing leads with all new prospect programs. Keep in mind that, even though the prospects are aware of your company, continual reminders, sometimes referred to as "touches," are important.

Just be sure you "touch" them in appropriate ways and don't overextend your welcome. Make all communications in the context of how you met or the reason why you are contacting them so you won't confuse or concern anyone.

Marketing methods that are common to help foster leads toward the ultimate purchase decision include:

Brochures

- Typically an overview of your company, products, and services
- Can be done online or on paper (or both)
- Online may involve animation, audio, video, or other computer-based interactions

- The quality of paper and the imagery or artwork that you use can contribute to the image

Datasheets, Product/Service Information Sheets, and Spec Sheets

- Depending on the business, datasheets can provide additional detailed information that is otherwise too much to include in a brochure. Some companies use a brochure to talk about the company at large, and then create more detailed product or service information sheets.

- Using a datasheet may be useful to separate product or service specifications for specific types of prospects or to present information that is often changing. By using a datasheet for such details, you update the datasheet and not the more expensive brochure.

Whitepapers and Briefs

- Usually written on a relevant technical topic, market trend, or controversial issue, whitepapers are research writings that provoke consideration about a topic or present a viewpoint. They are ideally written without mentioning your own product or service except as an example or at the end as a credit. Usually there is an "About the Company" at the very end of the document.

- Whitepapers rank high on customer use, especially in the world of Business-to-Business information sharing. Often, companies will offer whitepapers as free downloads from their websites. They can be a good way to bring people to your website and educate them. There is a high correlation to whitepapers and viral marketing in that customers often pass these along as they are informative and non-commercial. If you do offer whitepapers for free download, request that prospects provide their contact information before they can download a given document. You also want to include language in that process that clearly says they are opting-in to any future contact.

- Some companies produce e-Books or e-Briefs made available as PDFs for regular download or available through online book sellers such as Amazon.com. Amazon, for example, has some new programs to encourage e-Book (Kindle) production and consumption and many others are likely to follow.

Website(s)

- Your website should reflect the messaging and materials you offer as determined by your marketing inventory.

- Depending on your business, your website may be sophisticated or simple. Flashiness is impressive but may not influence prospects (or in some cases turn them off). Most importantly, make the navigation easy to follow and the information relevant, up-to-date, accurate, and well presented.

Blogs and Online Discussion Groups

- Far from new, online discussion groups are virtual meeting spaces where people can post topics, answer fellow member questions, or simply browse the archives of discussions. Setup and management is easy and inexpensive, sometimes even free – e.g., Yahoo, Google's Groups, or Gather Groups. I have even seen some companies set up topical discussion boards that they don't participate in actively. Rather, the company uses it to learn from the members. In this way, they can see what the top issues are and look for potential leads. You don't even have to set up your own discussion group for this if there are those already out there that prospects and customers use.

- Blogs are a more recent phenomenon. They are a popular way to create public online diaries about individuals or companies. Blogging success definitely depends on the interests of the audience in that topic and the connection and talent of the writer. There are still many arguments among marketers whether blogs help sell products directly or if they simply help with search engine optimization (SEO). Successful blogs are updated frequently, which certainly requires human resources. Because blogs can include public comments (people can post inappropriate content), the blog may need to be moderated and managed. There are many tools available that help you create a blog for free or for a low cost. There is also a tremendous amount of information on how to optimize a blog and utilize the blogosphere to promote your blog. More often than not, marketing efforts go into getting other influential bloggers to write about your products or services much like any other media format.

Videos

- If a picture is worth 1000 words, video is definitely undervalued. Video has long been a great way to gain someone's attention and increase comprehension. Digital videos (especially educational or how-to types) can be sent via email, via CD/DVD in the mail, used at tradeshows or other events, embedded in websites, and uploaded on YouTube and other public video servers.

- Video on the web (often called a screencast) is being used more and more to help educate consumers using an oh-so familiar and effective medium. Web video links can be emailed to create a viral buzz. Unlike textual formats, web videos are often preferred by both people and search engines.

- Creating videos for your website can be relatively easy and cost effective.

This does not mean they should be silly or sloppy, because web video viewers prefer honest and real productions, and even shun those that are too slick and less credible. I am not suggesting producing a corporate video using your cell phone camera, but the plethora of hardware and software enables almost anyone to inexpensively produce a decent quality web video.

Customer Case Studies

- Case studies are often the most valuable material for prospects to learn how and why others benefited from your offering. Case studies are easy to create and publish. They can be posted on your website and others' sites. The studies can be distributed via email (as a file or a link to the posted file) and used in marketing materials such as brochures and advertisements. You can produce your case studies in video too. Both prospects and media love case studies and they are great ways for you to learn more about your customers too!

Cost and ROI Estimation Tools

- Depending on your product or service, you may be able to help prospects utilize an online tool or do-it-yourself formula to see their forecasted costs or return on investment (ROI) in terms of dollars and time. ROI is a measurement that compares the amount a customer pays for your product or service and how much they receive back in terms of additional revenue or savings. "Breakeven" is also useful in some sales situations as it identifies when the cost of the product or service is equal to the gain. This shows someone how long it should take before their investment in purchasing your offering will provide them financial value back. In Chapter 5, we outlined some questions to ask customers that will help you to determine the ROI from your product or services. Providing this information to prospects may help speed the sales cycle so providing tools to your salespeople and/or prospects is usually a great marketing asset. Also consider the type of online tools often found on auto insurer websites or banks and mortgage providers. With simple input, prospects can calculate important financials for themselves such as monthly payments, lifetime payments, or comparative payment plans. These assist prospects to consider various ways to pay for the product or service which can speed up a sales cycle toward closure.

Demos

- Depending on your product or service, it may be appropriate to have a demonstration available for your prospects. Demos can be available on your website as a self-running "canned" demo or you may require prospects to set up a date and time that a company representative can go through a demo with the prospect online or in person. There are all kinds of demos varying in terms of length, content, format, and so on. The key with demos is trying to keep them as short and organized as possible. It's a great idea if you can give users the ability to customize and drive the demo to best suit their particular interests. Always require prospects to sign up and provide contact information in exchange for the demo.

Presentations

- Your sales people and customers may want to utilize a set of presentation slides. Presentations can be projected, or distributed as a paper handout. Presentations can cover information about the company and your offerings and should clearly explain your positioning. Strive for a professional look and feel and one that compliments your image. You may include speaker notes or scripts to ensure that the other people in your organization can deliver the presentation effectively.

Email and phone call follow-ups

- A simple email or phone call (even if only voicemail) to follow up with a prospect can be very effective. The message should be specific to the prospect's prior experience such as "thank you for visiting our booth at the XYZ tradeshow," or "thank you for viewing our online demo." Always state the call to action for the next step such as, "please call me back to schedule a meeting," or "please join us for our next webinar." You might also include pointers to additional information that you have available on your website or other sites. Keep in mind the insights gained in the marketing inventory within the buying process section. Take this opportunity to move the prospect along to the next step!

Grassroots Marketing

- Many marketing success stories come from grassroots efforts.

This is a catch-all phrase for programs that are very local, cost little or nothing to do and help generate word-of-mouth buzz about a product or service. Activities might include handing out flyers at a local event or emailing information to friends and family and asking them to send it on to their family and friends. Going door-to-door and visiting local venues to promote your offering may allow you to interact with important prospects and supporters.

This is by no means a complete list of lead fostering program ideas, but these are the most common types. Apply as much creativity as you can, but be sure to apply your marketing inventory answers to ensure the right information is being delivered to the right people in the right way.

For example, don't depend on email if your prospects don't have access to the internet during work hours. And most importantly, be sure to consider how you can measure success of any program so at the very least, you can evaluate whether to invest in a similar one again!

Lead Management

As noted before, obtaining leads is only half the challenge. The other half is following up. Ideally, you should determine a lead path for all prospects. That is, once they "find" you at a trade show or from your website, have an established plan of follow-up. In larger organizations with Customer Relationship Management (CRM) or Marketing Automation Systems, the systems can assist with lead follow-up by issuing rule-based emails assigned to appropriate employees. In smaller organizations, you can still have a process in place for responding to the different types of marketing channels. For events, you may have a certain employee call to follow-up with all leads gathered. For website inquiries, you can have someone send an email or call the prospect. If you have a store or other place of business where prospects might "show up," perhaps you should have a process to welcome the prospect and get their basic contact information so they can be followed up after they leave the shop. If you think about all the ways someone might find your company, you can create a process for following up. The processes don't need to be difficult or time consuming. In fact, once you create the initial email or other follow-up process, you should be able to reuse it over and over again with little modification.

**Ⓘ No Time
30 MIN TO-DO**

Lead Follow-up Plan

For each source of leads, note the person or system that is responsible for follow-up, and when and what they should do.

Lead Source	Person or system responsible for follow- up; specify what and when follow-up is desired
Example: website form	*Automated website email to be issued immediately upon form being submitted by prospects; then again five days later... Mary in telesales will call to follow up. If voicemail left and no reply from prospect, Mary to call again in five days. If able to talk with prospect, Mary will pass interested lead to Joe in Sales. If prospect is not interested, Mary will note in lead tracking system as 'not interested.'*
Website form	
Email inquiries	
Call in	

Walk in	
Tradeshow	
Direct mail reply	
Webinars	
In person seminars	
Telemarketing lead	

Tracking Leads

Tracking leads could be a book unto itself and a few have already been written. Larger organizations often use sales or marketing automation systems (e.g. Salesforce.com and Siebel). Among other features, these systems can help track and coordinate leads across the organization. Smaller businesses usually don't have the luxury to track huge numbers of leads in sophisticated databases. You can, however, use Microsoft Excel, ACT!, Actionize.com, or similar less sophiticated solutions.

Ideally you want to track prospects' contact information, all the follow-ups that have been done, and the next needed step(s). Make it your own process to review the database every Monday morning to see what follow-up actions need to happen that week. If you assigned a "task" to another employee, find out where those things are and note them in the database. Not only does this database help keep your leads moving forward, but it can be the ultimate source for understanding your prospects' buying cycles, and to identify which marketing programs are working and which are not. Over time, you'll even be able to calculate ROI on individual programs and your overall marketing plan.

You now have the information and plan for who, what and how to market to the appropriate prospects and what to do with them once you get their attention. Next, you need a quick and easy way to pull this all together so you can see the whole picture and gain the approval of your company colleagues. But, like everyone these days, your colleagues also have limited attention so we'll discuss in the next chapter how to smartly present all of this valuable information to your colleagues.

*There's no time to write.
Package and present your marketing
plans concisely, precisely.*

Chapter 8:
Don't Write, Present!

In today's entertaining visual world of video, I am a big believer that few people actually read any more than they are required for survival or pleasure. Because marketing plans are usually not considered required reading, I don't recommend slaving over a long document. While I personally love a well written Marketing Requirements Document (MRD) and other elegant marketing plans, in reality, we just don't have time to prepare or appreciate these as the market keeps moving swiftly ahead.

It is, however, very effective for you to present a summary of your marketing plan and dialogue about your plan with people who can quickly provide you with challenging questions and honest feedback. This will help you validate your assumptions and allow you to justify the marketing decisions to yourself and others. The goal here is to summarize the plan into a short, under 30-minute presentation that can be delivered to selected individuals who you feel will provide valuable feedback.

First, consider for just five minutes to whom you will present your finished plan. List as many individuals that you feel will provide you valuable, unique feedback. You can present individually or in small groups, but don't present just one time. Be sure to have at least three instances where you can present the plan. This allows for individual feedback and allows you to see how well your ideas are communicated to different people. It also gives you the opportunity to hone your presentation and the plan as you obtain incremental feedback and experience.

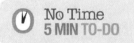

My Presentation Review Plans

Note whom you will present your draft plan to and mark it when it is completed:

Reviewer's Name   **Note Date Presentation**
Done

_____   Done _____

_____   Done_____

_____   Done _____

_____   Done _____

_____   Done _____

_____   Done _____

_____   Done _____

_____   Done _____

No Time
30 MIN TO-DO

Fill in the Presentation Template

You should use all the information you now know from your marketing inventory and positioning work to fill in the template on the next few pages. This presentation template is also available online at   www.NoTimeMarketing.com/presentationtemplate.

Notes:
- *Comments are noted on slides with italics in reduced font size*
- *Always state the source of your data, especially that coming from your marketing inventory research*

Slide 1:

Marketing Plan

_____

[Your Company Name]

_____

[date]

Our Customers

- We sell to _____
  (B to B or B to C?, what typical size, type of company?)

- Our customers are: _____
  _____
  (describe demographics and other descriptive info)

- The person that ultimately buys our offering
  is:_____
  (title/type, preferences, demographics, etc.)

- The person(s) that uses our offering is/are:
  _____
  (title/type, preferences, demographics, etc.)

- The person(s) that influence a purchase decision
  is/are: _____
  (title/type, preferences, demographics, etc.)

- In addition to the current market, we'd like to sell to:
  _____
  (new geographies, industries, people)

Slide 3:

Our Competition

- The following companies sell a similar product/service:
  _____

- Other ways users can accomplish the same function are:
  _____

- Our solution is unique and better because:
  _____

- Our weaknesses are: _____

- The risks someone has not using our solution are:
  _____

- Relative to our competition, we are priced:
  _____

- I admire the following companies' marketing:
  _____

Slide 4:

The Buying Process

- A typical buying process for our product/service is:

  _____

  _____

- The buying cycle is typically _____
  days/months/years

- Prospects require the following processes and materials
  before making a decision:

  _____   _____

  _____

  (e.g. RFP, demo, references, trial, etc.)

- When purchasing our offering, customers can do it:

  _____

  (anytime, only during a budget cycle)

- We win deals _____ % of the time.

Slide 5:

Our Marketing Channels

- Our prospects and customers typically read/watch/listen to:_____

- They do this _____ *(at home? at work?)*

- They go to these tradeshows/conferences:
  _____
  _____

- They belong to these associations/clubs:
  _____
  _____
  _____

- The industry thought leaders are:
  _____
  _____

Slide 6:

Our Market

- The key trends in our industry are:

  _____

  _____

- This is a _____ *(crowded, open)* market.

- Our short term market share goals are:

  _____

  _____

- Our long term market share goals are:

  _____

  _____

- Over time, we want to be known as:

  _____

  _____

Slide 7:

Positioning

_____

(Your Company)

provides

_____

(Describe product/service)

that

_____

(Describe benefit of using your product/service instead of alternative means to address the problem)

_____

_____.

Unlike other solutions, our product

_____.

(Compared to the competition, describe your unique selling proposition)

Slide 8:

Marketing Message

- In our messaging, we want to be described as:

  _____

  (from your marketing messaging exercises)

- We want to embody: _____
  (note dream celebrity spokesperson)

- We want our company image to be more like :

  _____

  (note other companies admired)

Slide 9:

Pricing

Our product/service unit cost   =   _____

Our customer's price   =   _____

The highest price competition   =   _____

The lowest price competition   =   _____

Our current price   =   _____

Our current margin   =   _____

Our desired price   =   _____

Our desired margin   =   _____

Slide 10:

Generating Leads

The programs I will do to generate new leads for the company are:

_____

_____

_____

_____

_____

_____

I will measure lead success by:

_____

_____

_____

Leads will be followed up as follows:

_____

_____

_____

_____

Chapter 9:
Last Thoughts

My hope is that you have learned a lot about marketing, about your business and how to generate more profitable sales. The world moves very fast and while many people would love to cross all the T's and dot all the I's, it isn't always practical – especially in resource deprived businesses.

> *The overabundance of information from our hyper-connected world is wonderfully helpful, but it is also numbing to most busy people.*

We are exposed to so much information all the time. As a result, we have little time or ability to think, plan, or execute on anything except "top of the pile" matters. As such, I hope this book has cut through some of the clutter and helped you understand essential marketing concepts that you can apply to your business – immediately and effectively.

I thank you for reading this book and I encourage you, if you haven't already, to check www.NoTimeMarketing.com for additional information on our ongoing teleconsulting, presentations and workshops.

Your Feedback!

By filling in our online feedback form, you will be entered into our monthly drawing that awards three individuals a free 30 minute marketing consultation via phone:

www.NoTimeMarketing/feedback

*Things marketing professors
will never tell you!*

Alyssa's Marketing Truths

1. Marketing is as much an art as it is a science. Plan, test, execute, and measure, but never be surprised by uncertainty and change.

2. You usually need to bang on the same prospect door four or more times before someone answers. Make sure that you have the right address.

3. You are not your customer. Never assume you know them that well.

4. Restricted resources represent an opportunity to embrace creativity and revisit comfort.

5. Don't confuse prospect enthusiasm for purchase authority.

6. Motivate don't manipulate.

7. Quality precedes quantity.

8. The best teachers are students.

9. Confidence sells. BS smells.

10. Spend only if you would be willing to pick up the tab.

Even small businesses can appreciate the triple bottom line benefits of being a good corporate citizen.

Addendum I: Responsible Small Business Marketing

I would be remiss if I didn't discuss a bit about corporate social responsibility. Much of my consulting practice is dedicated to helping companies be more responsible in terms of their philanthropy, environmental initiatives, governance, and employee volunteer programs. Corporate social responsibility (CSR) is not really a new concept but one escalated by economic and political factors including Al Gore's *Inconvenient Truth*, the 2008 financial crisis created by Wall Street, a lack of governmental regulation, and a new generation of workers that have redefined success in terms of contribution to family, Earth, and cause.

As such, I do not believe CSR is a fad or likely to go away soon. Comparable to the quality movement in the 80's and 90's, it will take some time before CSR is engrained in corporate culture. Short term, CSR is a competitive advantage that leading companies can temporarily exploit as a sales and marketing opportunity. However, I do believe that soon, the question will change from "what you are doing to be a good corporate citizen", to rather, "can you afford not to be a great one."

Let us discuss briefly what corporate citizenship is all about, and subsequently how it should and can impact small businesses today.

In addition to differing monikers (e.g. CSR, corporate citizenship, and sustainability), there are several definitions of corporate citizenship. Some definitions come from academic institutions and some from corporate-member organizations. I use a definition that fits in with existing corporate structure and function to make it easier to relate and implement. My definition reflects the components of corporate social responsibility to include:

- *Philanthropy* – Often managed by foundations or trusts, corporate giving can be in the form of cash or in-kind donations. In-kind donations may include physical goods such as furniture, supplies, and office space but can also include volunteered services by employees or even former employees (e.g. retirees). Employee volunteerism may be encouraged by providing paid time off or simply done off company paid hours. Employees may volunteers at shelters, at fund raisers, or by providing their skills such as accounting, marketing, or management. Executives often hold voluntary board seats on non-profit organizations.

  I also put cause marketing in this category which includes companies that sponsor events or initiatives through non-profits or non-governmental organizations (NGOs). Think of this as a company buying the rights to put their name or brand on a walk for hunger, homeless shelter, food drive, or other fund raising program.

- *Environmental sustainability and protection* – For me, sustainability is all about replenishing the natural resources that are used as well as minimizing the impact on the environment. This would include reducing your carbon footprint as well as recycling. I separate "protection" to indicate avoiding usage of a natural resource in the first place. For example, if you run a paper company, rather than cutting down and then replanting trees, protection would mean finding alternative means to making paper with recycled or alternative, less destructive materials.

  Environmental stewardship runs into: (1) the corporate and field offices, (2) in the manufacturing process (even service businesses often utilize goods that are made for them such as business cards, billing statements and other deliver supplies), and (3) in the consumer use of end goods. Companies should realize their overall environmental impact in these areas, and most obviously consider how to reduce, reuse, and recycle wherever possible.

- *Ethical investing* – Ethical investing includes the financial resources that flow into and out of the company and applying them in ethical ways. For example, a company that makes healthy products should not use its profits to invest in tobacco stocks. More and more we are seeing groups of investors that scrutinize the responsibility of companies before putting their large investment capital into such companies. Wall Street already has a number of indices to rank companies and I expect many more that reach beyond environmental measures. Independent auditors provide responsible rankings much like bond ratings and media publications develop top 100 lists of the "best" corporate citizens.

- *Corporate governance and ethics* – Beyond Sarbanes-Oxley, companies are being challenged to create and maintain ethics statements that extend throughout the organization, its subsidiaries and through the supply chain to partners. We are starting to see more companies offer CSR-specific annual reports that include either industry metrics such as the Global Reporting Initiative (GRI) and/or self-assessment means. As more reporting standards come to market, we are also seeing more CSR reports being professionally audited and being a key part of all annual shareholder meeting presentations. With record numbers of shareholder resolutions being filed that revolve around responsibility issues, it is often in the company's best interest to address CSR proactively and utilize the opportunity to self-assess gaps and achievements before someone else from the outside does.

- *Employee satisfaction, diversity and human rights* – Key to attracting and retaining top talent, employee satisfaction has always been a top concern of management and HR professionals. However, with the shifting dominance of minorities in the U.S., diversity once again is forefront to ensure that companies utilize the innovation and connection of a diverse workforce to better serve a diverse consumer base. Employees not only contribute within a company but they often are the best evangelists and outward bound brand carriers. Further, ensuring the health and well being of the employee base is not only critical to reducing medical benefit expense to a company, but also helps to ensure the highest employee productivity.

- *Supplier diversity, support and accountability* – One of the most overlooked but possibly most critical areas of corporate responsibility lies with the supply chain. Visible cases such as Mattel, Gap, and additional otherwise respected brands have found that ignorance with partner practices can lead to huge damages to the company brand and sales. As such, more and more companies are examining and imposing CSR requirements to partners and suppliers, even to smaller companies. Consider the well publicized requirements of doing business with Wal-Mart. Being able to report and maintain responsibility reporting to such partners is already a requirement and is subsequently spreading to more and more brand name corporations.

With these tenets identified, it is clear that companies have much to worry about. I often say that CSR can be thought of as a due diligence process to identify liabilities and opportunities that otherwise aren't apparent in non-core areas. For example, manufacturing companies spend enormous resources honing their processes to ensure the highest levels of productivity and profit. Now they must also consider as part of their overall sales and business planning the waste generated, their impact on the communities in which they operate, their employee contributions inside and outside of the company, and the impact to the companies that they supply and that supply them. Regardless of the motivation to be better corporate citizens, companies are already striving to prove their worth to a variety of stakeholders that don't always value profit as the only company asset.

So how does this apply to smaller businesses? Clearly as a supplier or partner to a larger company that imposes CSR requirements on your company, this may cause you to do things differently or force you to report on aspects that were previously not captured. However, I hope the reasons you are reading this in the first place is that you are interested in being a better corporate citizen for the sake of "doing the right thing." Perhaps this will help you sleep better at night, or enable you to look your kids and grandkids more squarely in the eyes. Perhaps you view CSR as a competitive advantage or a way to better engage your consumers and community. Whatever your motivation, let me offer a few ideas to increase your corporate citizenship that are easy, quick, and cost effective.

1. <u>Utilize an employee CSR committee.</u> – If you have more than 3 employees, you can probably find someone who would love to chair a committee to identify ways for the business to reduce, reuse, and recycle. Make sure the committee has executive visibility (if not direct participation) and, if possible, support the group financially with an operating budget, even if small to start. Highlight the work of the committee in internal communications and even outside PR which is good for the committee as it is the company.

2. <u>Encourage employee volunteerism.</u> – Even if you cannot offer paid time off, encourage employee volunteerism by setting the example yourself and with your fellow managers. Write up the work being done in the company newsletter or Intranet. Have a special volunteer luncheon or other similar recognition program. Work with the organizations that are receiving the volunteer contributions to figure out ways to optimize your company's involvement and do joint PR.

3. <u>Give to local causes</u> – If possible, set aside some after tax profit to give to causes that are relevant to your employees, customers and other stakeholders. You can find out which causes simply asking them! Typical corporate giving is 1%

of pre-tax profit but any amount is honorable. If this is done through an employee committee, it can be even better so that the recognition is spread through bottom-up means and not top down management horn blowing.

4. <u>Add CSR questions to your sourcing.</u> – Think about all the goods and services your company buys and start asking your suppliers about where everything comes from and what standards are used to ensure that they are properly produced. If you hire a cleaning company, do you know if the workers are getting a fair wage? Are they using safe cleaning products? Do your copier, onsite printers and professional print shop partners utilize recycled paper? Do your employees have a way to easily recycle paper and other items in their offices and eating areas? Can your landlord replace bathroom appliances with low flow and auto-shut off devices? Do you offer your employees who drink coffee and water the ability to use recyclable or reusable cups? With so many opportunities and questions, this is an area your employee committee can really focus on to look for ways to find small but powerful solutions.

While I've pointed to mostly management issues and not specific marketing ones, marketing plays a key role in effective corporate social responsibility. The most obvious contribution is doing transparent, accurate reporting of activities and being mindful of the difference between promotion and communication. There is a clear line between bragging and informing. Goodwill efforts will get immediately bruised by overt promotion or inaccurate communication. Marketers must realize this when they communicate CSR activities on websites, press releases, brochures, reports, and other collaterals. *Marketing spin is the cancer of effective CSR.*

Claims must be substantiated by real data and ideally, third party endorsement. And perhaps most importantly, marketing must have an appreciation of the resources to be utilized for marketing campaigns. This means considering beforehand: the paper and/electricity that a planned mailing campaign may require; recognizing the visibility and usage differences between print advertising versus billboards; segmenting the prospect market even better to spend resources to reach only those that care and will act rather than trying to hit a few birds with lots of wasted pebbles; and scrutinizing where promotional items and services are being built and by whom. Fair wages and ethical workforce management must be confirmed by the vendors that supply marketers with goods and services. With some promotional items, it is also important to check the safety tests and standards as no marketer wants to find out that their promotional giveaway has literally been recalled by the National Safety Commission (NSC). NSC recalls have already cost some very otherwise reputable brands a lot of money in paying fees, fighting litigations, and restoring their corporate image. This isn't the type of recall that marketing wants!

In summary, companies of all sizes are moving toward being more socially responsible for their actions and marketing. Whether used as a competitive advantage or liability avoidance, corporate citizenship is in everyone's best interest.

Acknowledgements

It really does take a village to write a book! As such, I'd like to thank the many people who helped to inspire and create this book.

First, to my colleague, Peter Fingar, who understands and practices being a real business partner. He is the quintessential technologist, teacher, cynic and most of all, a friend who I will always appreciate tremendously. Next, my lifelong business partner, Marco Emrich, who is always there with his opinion, his love and his cell phone into which I complain about things well beyond my allowance. Without his ongoing, unconditional support, there are many things that I wouldn't be able to do, including this book.

I had many friendly editors helping with early versions of the book that I'd like to acknowledge: Jen McNeil, Gail Wertheimer, Beth Rocco, Brian Lawley, Jameel Webb-Davis, Ray Graber, Marilyn Krause Babb, and Lynn Toomey.

Thank you to Andrew Swain for making my photo shoot painless and to Jackrabbit Design for their work on the cover and website.

Index

INSPIRED

A Bible Companion for Teens

MARK HART

Authored by Mark Hart

Cover design by David Calavitta
Interior design by Ryan McQuade

Copy editing by Elizabeth Bayardi

Published by Life Teen, Inc. 2222 S. Dobson Rd. Suite 601 Mesa, AZ 85202
LifeTeen.com

TABLE OF CONTENTS

Making Scripture a Daily Prayer

Appendix

INTRODUCTION

There it sits: big, intimidating, and one might even say "*old*." But calling the Bible old is actually a little short-sighted. While the writings are old, it would probably be more accurate to call it *ancient* since the word "old" usually has a negative connotation associated with it. When we say the Bible is ancient, however, it can mean many things. Ancient as in "it comes from a different time or place," yes, but also as in it has survived countless centuries and assaults against it.

Written in more languages, read by more people, with more copies published and sold than any other written work in the history of the world, the Holy Bible stands alone. Kings and rulers have tried to outlaw it, wars have been waged over it, and millions of lives have been lost but also found because of it. God's divine revelation: inspired, recorded, entrusted, and gifted to us. And although the Bible is often judged by its cover and let's be honest, the covers of many Bibles are pretty un-inspiring, no other book will ever compare. Seventy-three books, inspired by God and recorded over a span of about 1,700 years by more than 40 separate authors, the Bible is one of our greatest family heirlooms.

Consider a starry sky, a sunset on the ocean, or a baby's laughter. Assuredly, the creator is seen throughout His gorgeous creations, but God's revelation is not limited to nature. God declares His love and providence in a myriad of ways and just as freely as He reveals Himself to us through created things, so He does through His inspired Word. God's plan for our salvation is played out age-after-age, from the dawn of history. But the danger for modern believers is when we fail to see history as just that: *His story*. Even more dangerous is when we don't understand that our stories are found in and wrapped up in God's.

As Pope Francis reminded us, "So this love story began, a story that has gone on for so long, and is not yet ended. We, the women and men of the Church, we are in the middle of a love story: each of us is a link in this chain of love. And if we do not understand this, we have understood nothing of what the Church is." [1]

Consider this: Jesus Christ could have chosen to teach us in a variety of ways. He could have stuck with only long sermons using such big words that even the greatest minds, like St. Thomas Aquinas, would have appeared as nothing more than gurgling babies in comparison. The fact that the second person of the Trinity chose to employ story-telling (parables) as His primary teaching tool tells us a great deal. Everyone loves a good story and our story is part of the greatest story ever told.

There's a reason the Bible has been translated into every conceivable language on Earth (even "Klingon" for you Star Trek fans). There's a reason that when Johannes Gutenberg — a Catholic — invented the printing press, his first print job was the Bible. There's a reason we paint our favorite verses on walls or scribble them in greeting cards. After thousands of years not even Hallmark can do better than "Love is patient. Love is kind," which is probably why they quote it so often. And although the works of Shakespeare and Austen and Hemingway are beautiful, and their characters are beloved, these authors were only masters of the written word — but Jesus is the living Word incarnate who came down from heaven. While inspired by life and love, these authors were not inspired in the same way as the authors of the Bible — not by the purest love of the Holy Spirit.

The Bible is prayer, the very breath and life of God. It is the Word of God, not mere words "about" God. That distinction necessitates our attention and demands reverence. That distinction should comfort you in your affliction and "afflict" you when you get too comfortable. The journey to God is about joy not happiness. Happiness is fleeting but joy — of a life in Christ and life in heaven — is eternal. We come to know that life in Christ through the sacraments and quite literally through the Scriptures, for only in knowing Christ do we come to know what it means to truly live.

WHY SCRIPTURE?

GETTING TO KNOW GOD

There are a lot of ways you can get to know someone: you can hear about them from someone else, you can check out their Snapchat or Instagram, or you can watch how they interact with other people. If they're famous, you might even watch a YouTube interview or read a blog about their life. None of these methods, though, are nearly as effective as actually sitting with the person, one-on-one, and asking them meaningful questions like:

Where did you grow up?
What was your childhood like?
What are you most afraid of?
What brings you the most joy?
Why do you do what you do?
How does it make you feel when...?
Who is your personal hero?
What roles do God and faith play in your life?

Questions like these help you get past shallow topics and allow you to really get to know a person; they reveal a person's true identity. While you can use these questions to get to know other people, they are also a great starting point for getting to know yourself.

Where does your identity come from? Where do your beliefs come from? What (or who) do you base your decisions on? These are all important questions to reflect on and they should all lead you back to one fundamental truth: You are not your own creator. You are the main character in your story, but you are not the author of your life.

God is the author of your life.

That's right, God is the author and you are a character in *His story*, not the other way around. Reality reveals (and the Bible affirms) that God created you through your parents. He loves you and wants you here. And if you really want to know yourself, the best and fastest way to do that is to get to know the one who created you.

The Bible is a great way to get to know God, the author of your story. By reading about His interactions with people who came before us, you not only learn about how God thinks and moves, but how others have responded to Him in both right and wrong ways.

When you read Scripture, you will see that while customs and traditions change, people don't really change all that much. You will realize that you have more in common with Biblical characters than you would have originally thought. We aren't just reading about people from thousands of years ago. No, when we read the Bible it's as though we're reading about ourselves. God doesn't change, so knowing what did and did not please Him then is a great way of knowing what does and does not please Him now.

In this Bible companion you are going to be introduced (or reintroduced) to God's Word in a variety of ways. You'll learn how to navigate the Scriptures, locating the chapter, verse, and specific stories. You'll be given an overview of different kinds of writings and styles, what to look for, and honestly, what you probably want to "avoid" as you begin reading. You'll be given practical examples, tools, and important insights so you can start to successfully pray the Bible on your own. Additionally, you'll be directed to dozens of passages and stories, some of which you might know well and others you might not recognize at all. Some are heroic and some are heartbreaking, but they're all thoroughly human. If you look hard enough, you might find a little bit of yourself in each story. At the very least, you'll be reintroduced to a God who is madly in love with you.

It's important to remember that while God might not love everything you do, He loves you and is cheering you on to your own sainthood. This companion will act as a small step in that direction. Some of the verses you'll find cited will convict you, some will challenge you, and many will affirm you. In the pages that follow, the Holy Spirit will meet you where you're at and inspire you to look deeper, further, and higher.

The characters and stories from Sacred Scripture all have something worth imitating and learning, so stop and learn from them. What you'll soon realize is that living as a Christian is not so much about "finding yourself," as it is about finding and unleashing Christ's presence and power within you. The more you recognize God's presence — in you, your family, your school, the Church, the world — the better you'll be able to share His love with all those you come in contact with.

The secret to a joyful life and a hope-filled future isn't about figuring out tomorrow, it's about listening to God today. God, the author of life, has something to say to you through the brothers and sisters who came before you. If you want to know God better, take a deep breath and turn the page.

It's story time.

OUR TYPICAL CATHOLIC
EXPERIENCE OF SCRIPTURE

The opening music has ended (hopefully on the correct note). The priest has recited the opening prayer. We have punched ourselves in the chest while uttering the Latin phrase *"mea culpa."* A kind-looking, elderly woman in a flower-print dress walks up to the ambo (the podium that holds the book of readings) and adjusts the microphone, sending an awful sound and nerve-wracking shockwaves down every Mass-goers' spine.

"A Reading from Second Kings," she proclaims in a monotone voice, eliciting neither excitement nor familiarity from 99 percent of the souls in the pews. She continues with a passage such as this:

"But every nation still made gods of its own, and put them in the shrines of the high places which the Samaritans had made, every nation in the cities in which they dwelt; the men of Babylon made Suc'coth-be'noth, the men of Cuth made Nergal, the men of Hamath made Ashi'ma, and the Av'vites made Nibhaz and Tartak; and the Sephar'vites burned their children in the fire to Adram'melech and Anam'melech, the gods of Sepharva'im. They also feared the Lord, and appointed from among themselves all sorts of people as priests of the high places, who sacrificed for them in the shrines of the high places."

At this point, even Biblical scholars have a headache. If you were able to track the reading for even the first 15 seconds, you probably began wondering, *"Is it God's plan to torture me? Why am I hearing this? What could this possibly have to do with my life?!?"*

Then the kind lady utters, "The Word of the Lord" to the congregation. We respond, "Thanks be to God" in a tone that sounds more like gratitude for the painful reading coming to an end than a prayer.

It was usually at this point — after the first reading (from the Old Testament) and before the song (which is a psalm, also from the Bible) — that I would completely zone out. I believed God and the Church had nothing for me and could not be more disassociated from my reality, so I stopped listening.

The truth is that I'm not the only person who has ever felt this way and if you've ever shared this feeling, you're not alone. It doesn't make you horrible, it makes you human.

But, here's the thing: A reading or passage from the Old Testament (or anywhere in Scripture, for that matter) may not appear to have any point or purpose or anything to do with your life, but there is always something you can take away from it.

God's Word is timeless truth and nothing in Scripture is there by "accident." The Bible was inspired by the Holy Spirit, so the writing is intentional and purposeful. That being said, since we are reading about ancient cultures in foreign lands, many of the facts and details — in order to be properly understood — require context.

This is where people go wrong.

Often times people focus only on the *content*, the who, what, when, and where of a story. The problem with this being the sole focus, however, is that it fails to take into consideration the original authors' intended meaning and audience, as well as their cultural perspective and idiomatic expressions. We, as Catholics, are blessed to have sacred tradition, which helps us "read out" the intended meaning of a passage (a term called *exegesis*) rather than "read into" a passage with our own cultural biases. Put more simply, the Catholic perspective offers us *context* — which gives us information (content), but also shows us how all of the content (the who, what, when, and where) is woven together (context) into the picture of salvation history. Context gives us a bigger perspective; it speaks to the "why."

At first hearing, then passage from 2 Kings could not be more confusing as it mentions gods and lands we are not familiar with in the 21st century. However, if we know or learn a little Biblical history and the time period it is set in, we realize this story offers us timeless truth. Interestingly enough, this passage comes from a period in which the northern kingdom of Israel had been overrun by the king of Assyria. Israel's king at the time was a despicable and cowardly man who turned his back on the one, true God. As a result, the king of Assyria (who believed in many gods) overthrew Israel, enslaved many, killed many more, and settled in Samaria (Israel's capital) with many Assyrians who brought their worship of false gods with them. In this reading, we hear of some of the horrid practices that took place — Assyrians worshipping their false gods and murdering their innocent children, burning them alive as part of their idol worship.

Can you imagine a culture or society that does not protect the innocent lives of children? Can you imagine what terrible things happen when people stop worshipping the one, true God and begin worshipping false gods or, worse yet, themselves? Of course you can. Even in the 21st century, we see what happens when people turn their backs on God, truth, and the dignity of human life. This is just one example of verses that may seem "outdated" or purposeless to us upon first hearing but that, after further examination, prove to be timeless in their wisdom.

Still, it takes time to learn the backstory, history, and context. You may be thinking, *"That's great, but what does the Bible have to say to me about everything I have going on in my life today?"*

Let's take a step back and try an exercise.

First, take a deep breath and clear your mind of all distractions.

Next, make the Sign of the Cross. Invite the Holy Spirit, the author of Scripture, to be with you and open your eyes, mind, and heart to what He wants to speak to you, this day.

Pray, "Come Holy Spirit" several times. Then pray through the verses that follow until you find one that "speaks" to your heart. Once you find one, read and pray through it several times.

GOD "VERSES" US

"Let no one despise your youth, but set the believers an example in speech and conduct, in love, in faith, in purity."
– 1 Timothy 4:12

"Not every one who says to me, 'Lord, Lord,' shall enter the kingdom of heaven, but he who does the will of my Father who is in heaven." – Matthew 7:21

"If the world hates you, know that it has hated me before it hated you. If you were of the world, the world would love its own; but because you are not of the world, but I chose you out of the world, therefore the world hates you." – John 15:18-19

"Truly, I say to you, whoever does not receive the kingdom of God like a child shall not enter it." – Mark 10:15

"No temptation has overtaken you that is not common to man. God is faithful, and he will not let you be tempted beyond your strength, but with the temptation will also provide the way of escape, that you may be able to endure it." – 1 Corinthians 10:13

"You shall love the Lord your God with all your heart, and with all your soul, and with all your mind, and with all your strength." – Mark 12:30

"Finally, be strong in the Lord and in the strength of his might." – Ephesians 6:10

"Take heed to yourselves; if your brother sins, rebuke him, and if he repents, forgive him." – Luke 17:3

"My lips will shout for joy, when I sing praises to thee; my soul also, which thou hast rescued." – Psalm 71:23

"Then our mouth was filled with laughter and our tongue with shouts of joy; then they said among the nations, 'The Lord has done great things for them.'"
– Psalm 126:2

"Count it all joy, my brethren, when you meet various trials." – James 1:2

"Whoever hates reproof walks in the steps of the sinner, but he that fears the Lord will repent in his heart."
– Sirach 21:6

"Without having seen him you love him; though you do not now see him you believe in him and rejoice with unutterable and exalted joy." – 1 Peter 1:8

"O God, from my youth thou hast taught me, and I still proclaim thy wondrous deeds." – Psalm 71:17

Now, ask yourself these questions:

- Why did this verse jump out at me today?

- Did any of the other verses also stand out to me?

- How is it that something written thousands of years ago can still speak to me, today?

- What difference does it make that these words come from God and not just a human author?

- What is God trying to tell me today about Himself, His love, or my life through this verse?

Now, read through the verse again and try to commit it to memory. You can go back to it daily or weekly, too. You'll probably find that, in time, other verses will begin to jump out and speak to you as well. Timeless truth has a funny way of never becoming outdated.

IS THE BIBLE RELIABLE READING?

The hotel room was pitch black. The air conditioner was on full blast. I was surrounded by pillows and hibernating in a cocoon-like fashion. I was perfectly comfortable so, of course, it was at that moment that I had to pee.

I began to navigate the foreign surroundings in the dark, making my way to the bathroom when, "WHAM!" I discovered a large dresser in my path. I yelped and fell back onto the bed. I'm not certain but it's quite likely that the word "shin" is Latin for "to find furniture in the dark."

It was at that moment, writhing in pain and wishing for death, that I recalled the famous passage from the Book of Psalms:

"Thy word is a lamp to my feet and a light to my path."
– Psalm 119:105

If only I had taken advantage of the light, I could have avoided so much pain.

But, the passage is teaching us more than that by reminding us that if more people sought the Word of God (Jesus Christ) in His Word (the Bible), they wouldn't be trapped in darkness (sin), blindly stumbling through life.

The Scriptures are meant to be a light. They are designed to not only guide us through darkness but also to beckon others to safety. They reveal God's plan, speak truth, and challenge us to change. God's Word, while timeless, offers timely wisdom for any circumstance or challenge we face. Basically, the Father loved us so much that He gave us His Word (the compass) and His Church (the guide), refusing to orphan His children in a wilderness of sin and immorality.

Still, there are countless people who argue that the Bible is "unreliable" or "outdated." Many people — some of whom are well read and quite intellectual — do everything they can to debunk the validity of Scripture, thinking that if they can exploit seeming "inconsistencies" or supposed "errors," they can somehow do away with Christianity and God. That's the first mistake.

When Theology is "Out of Order"

Saying, "The Bible has some things I don't agree with, so the Church must be wrong and God, therefore, is 'unloving' or 'not real' (or whatever else)" is completely backward. Faith doesn't begin with the Bible. You don't use the Bible to prove God's existence — that's like using the music of Nikki Minaj or One Direction to "prove" God hates me.

No, we begin with God. Once a soul believes in God, there's a decision to make regarding whether or not Jesus is God. Then, one must determine whether or not Christ instituted a Church. After that, one must understand that the Bible came out of a living Church (not vice versa).

The early Church — the first generation of eyewitness believers — was a Church of oral tradition that slowly gave us written tradition. That's one reason St. Paul is so quick to remind us to follow the Church (1 Timothy

3:15, 1 Corinthians 11:2, 2 Thessalonians 2:15). The Church didn't "come out of" the Bible, the Bible came out of Christ's Church.

Words Matter

We proclaim, as did the early Christians, that the Bible is the Word of God, not merely words "about" God. By the inspiration of the Holy Spirit, these words were written down to communicate the truth of the events that had occurred and were occurring.

Saint Luke, by his own admission, was not an eyewitness (although Matthew and John were) but received the truth of the events from eyewitnesses and ministers (Luke 1:2). He was so taken by the inexplicable reality of what he heard and saw, that he just had to write it down in an orderly way and share it (Luke 1:3). The truth was too good not to share (Luke 1:4). So, the question isn't, "Why did they feel the need to share this with all they encountered?" The real question is, "Why don't more people today have a passion to share it?"

"Modern" Snobs

The next mistake is when modern minds get snobbish, saying the Bible is "too outdated" or "not applicable" in our current culture. The notion that "old ideas" are not as solid as new ideas is not only senseless, it's dangerously prideful. In fact, old ideas are often far better because they've held up over time.

If you claimed to know better than a group of people in the modern age, you'd sound like a snob. Someone claiming to "know better'" than a group of people from the past really isn't any different. Yes, you have the internet, but they knew how to build pyramids without cranes, harvest crops without tractors, heal people without prescriptions, and chart stars without telescopes. Newer isn't always better and that idea applies to the Bible as well.

Angels are not Fairies

Some people try to dismiss the Bible because they say it's just fairy tales and myths. Not only are they denying the eyewitness accounts of countless souls who saw loaves multiplied, the dead raised, and the sea parted, they are also confusing different types of storytelling. Allegory was a popular form of storytelling, for instance. When the writers of Scripture, led and inspired by the Holy Spirit, used allegories as moral parables, they communicated truth, even if the truth was not literal.

The Church doesn't teach that God created everything in six, 24-hour periods. However, she does teach that everything was created by God with purpose. While the stories of creation may not be "scientifically accurate" as some scholarly types like to point out, it's important to note that Genesis was not written as a scientific account. The author(s) of Genesis sought to explain why God created, not "how." Saying Genesis scientifically proves God doesn't exist is like saying my love letter to my wife doesn't prove I exist or the phone book doesn't prove gravity is real; that was never their intended purpose!

Now, that's not to say that everything in the Bible is allegorical, far from it. Jesus healed the blind man, literally. He multiplied the loaves, literally. You can take additional symbolic or sacramental meaning out of the miracle, but it only enhances the physical, literal truth of the action. It's not an "either/or" but a "both/and" kind of miracle.

Finding Yourself in Scripture

Given all of this, some still wonder why we even need the Bible anymore. I mean, if we have our common sense, a conscience, and the Church, isn't the Bible — with all of its ancient, cultural references and accepted "ways of life" — kind of unnecessary?

If anything, we need the Bible more now than ever before. For instance, what if the God you think you know isn't the actual God, at all? Many people today follow a concept of Jesus that is not historically accurate — a pleasant, politically correct, "be nice to everyone" Jesus who is anything but Biblical. Many people ascribe traits to God that are not even remotely consistent with the God of Scripture.

In the Bible, you encounter the God of the universe and see how He moves, thinks, and speaks. You're not simply reading about characters from long ago, you're reading about your very self. The Bible isn't merely speaking to you; it's speaking about you. You are Adam and Eve, standing before God in all of your sin. You are Moses, worrying about your reputation. You are David, putting your wants before God's. You are Esther, deciding whether or not to endanger yourself in order to protect others. You are Peter, being called to lead even though you're far from perfect. You are the woman at the well, being told you have worth regardless of your past.

This is what the Bible offers you: an invitation to know God more deeply. The Bible helps you know God beyond just your head and engage Him in your heart. Scripture deepens your prayer, enlivens your worship, and makes the sacraments come to life in a whole new way.

WHY DO IT? THE GOAL OF READING THE BIBLE

What is the goal of reading the Bible, in general? There are far easier "self-help" books you can access and more readily understand, so why do you go to church or pray or take a few minutes to open up a book that is thousands of years old?

Well, since we're on the subject — and since the goal of this book is to help you begin to read and "get more" out of the Bible — let's let Scripture answer the question for us.

Turn to **1 Peter 1:9**.

What does it say is the "goal" of our faith?

The reason we "do" any and all of these faith-y, church-y things is the same: salvation. The reason we read the Bible, the reason we pray, the reason we go to Mass, the reason for every confession, rosary, act of service, and sacrament is the same — salvation. Notice, though, that the verse says, "the salvation of souls."

It's plural.

The goal of faith — and of reading the Bible — is not just for your salvation, but for the salvation of all. We have a responsibility to not only share a "what" (God's truth), but a "who" (God, Himself, in Jesus Christ). This is the reason we read the Bible, not merely to grow in knowledge of how God works or thinks or all He promises, but to grow in love for Him. Through Scripture, we learn how to die to ourselves (2 Corinthians 5:15) and let Christ shine in and through us (Galatians 2:20). So that's the goal of reading the Bible, that all might know Christ and experience salvation from sin and death — that all can come to know God and live with Him for eternity.

Now that you understand the overarching goal, you're going to need to desire to actually read the Bible. You'll need to know where to start as well as what books and sections to wait on until you develop some background and skills.

Let's begin at the beginning and get a feel for the Bible, as a whole, and how to navigate it before we start talking about which books to dive into and which (for now) to "avoid."

HOW IS THE BIBLE
ORGANIZED?

NAVIGATING THE BIBLE

The Bible is the most unique and unparalleled book in existence. Truthfully, though, it is not one book but many. The very word "bible" comes from the Latin word *biblia*, which means "collection of books" (think of the term "bibli-ography").

The Catholic Bible is comprised of 73 books and contains many different types of writing, including history, poetry, music, personal letters, visions, prophecies, advice, letters to communities of people, memoirs, allegories, and more.

THE BOOKS OF THE BIBLE
AND THEIR ABBREVIATIONS

The 73 Books of the Bible are broken into 46 Old Testament books that trace salvation history from creation until just before the birth of Christ. The 27 New Testament books begin with the four Gospels, which tell us of Christ's life, death, and Resurrection, and are followed by stories of the growth, challenges, persecutions, and successes of the early Church and the first Christian communities. The New Testament closes with the Book of Revelation, giving us insight into both the past and the future.

All of the books also have abbreviations to make it easier to cite them in books like this one or other works. The 73 Biblical books and their most common abbreviations are as follows:

Old Testament

Genesis – Gen

Exodus – Ex

Leviticus – Lev

Numbers – Num

Deuteronomy – Deut

Joshua – Josh

Judges – Judg

Ruth – Ruth

1 Samuel – 1 Sam

2 Samuel – 2 Sam

1 Kings – 1 Kings

2 Kings – 2 Kings

1 Chronicles – 1 Chr

2 Chronicles – 2 Chr

Ezra – Ezra

Nehemiah – Neh

Tobit - Tob

Judith – Jdt

Esther – Esth

1 Maccabees – 1 Macc

2 Maccabees – 2 Macc

Job – Job

Psalms – Ps(s)

Proverbs – Prov

Ecclesiastes – Eccl

Song of Songs – Song

Wisdom – Wis

Sirach – Sir

Isaiah – Isa

Jeremiah – Jer

Lamentations – Lam

Baruch – Bar

Ezekiel – Ezek

Daniel – Dan

Hosea – Hos

Joel – Joel

Amos – Am

Obadiah – Ob

Jonah – Jon

Micah – Mic

Nahum – Nah

Habakkuk – Hab

Zephaniah – Zeph

Haggai – Hag

Zechariah – Zech

Malachi – Mal

New Testament

Matthew – Mt

Mark – Mk

Luke – Lk

John – Jn

Acts of the Apostles – Acts

Romans – Rom

1 Corinthians – 1 Cor

2 Corinthians – 2 Cor

Galatians – Gal

Ephesians – Eph

Philippians – Phil

Colossians – Col

1 Thessalonians – 1 Thess

2 Thessalonians – 2 Thess

1 Timothy – 1 Tim

2 Timothy – 2 Tim

Titus – Titus

Philemon – Philem

Hebrews – Heb

James – Jas

1 Peter – 1 Pet

2 Peter – 2 Pet

1 John – 1 Jn

2 John – 2 Jn

3 John – 3 Jn

Jude – Jude

Revelation – Rev

How to Look Up a Bible Verse Using its Citation

It's possible you've never actually looked up a Bible verse before, but it's actually really easy. You may have seen the famous citation "John 3:16," for instance, on a poster in the end zone of a football field. You may have even seen "Jn 3:16." So, we know the "Jn" stands for the Gospel of John. The first number (before the colon) always references the chapter of the aforementioned book. You'll find the chapter numbers at the top of your Bible's pages and at the beginning of individual sections on each page. The second number (after the colon) stands for the verse. These are the smaller numbers you find within the text, separating thoughts and sentences.

So, when you see John 3:16, you'll turn to the New Testament (use the list on the previous page until you learn your way around the Old and New Testaments). Then you'll flip to chapter three (look at the top of the pages) and once in chapter three, look for the number "16" embedded within the text. There you'll find quite possibly the most famous verse in all of Sacred Scripture:

"For God so loved the world that he gave his only Son, that whoever believes in him should not perish but have eternal life." – John 3:16

NAVIGATING THE DIFFERENT TYPES OF BOOKS

Let's say you look up **Jn 3:16** and it seems to make sense. It's talking about Jesus, the cross, and God's plan to save us. It's read just as it was intended. It's clear. It's concise.

What if the next verse was **Prov 3:5-6** or **Rev 21:4-5**?

Go ahead and look them both up.

Now, do we understand them in the same way? All three verses teach us something about God, but they are different types of writing. In the Gospel of John, we have tales and details about Jesus' life and ministry. In Proverbs, we have what is called a "wisdom book," a book which, quite obviously, offers us wisdom. In Revelation, we have an "other" book that some list as prophetic, others apocalyptic, and still others, in a category all its own.

If you had to break the Bible down into only three "types" of books, they would be: history, wisdom, and prophecy. In other words, you can look at the past (historical), the present (wisdom), and the future (prophetic); or to put it more simply, where we've been, where we are, and where we're going.

The point being, we cannot fall into the trap of reading all of the books of the Bible in the same way. Some are meant to be read factually. Others are meant to be read allegorically or, even, metaphorically. Some are meant to communicate symbolism and others literalism.

Some people get annoyed with the first 11 chapters of Genesis because they aren't "scientific enough." They're looking for an exact "how" regarding the creation of the universe. The problem is that the author(s) of Genesis wasn't nearly as concerned about the "how" of creation as the "why." Looking for scientific facts while reading Genesis is like looking for a mathematic equation in a love letter — it's not the point of that type of writing.

Say you're writing a persuasive paper for your English class. The strategy you employ and points you make to support your thesis will look very different in this type of paper than they would in a compare/contrast paper, for instance. You, as the author, utilize different styles and strategies to make different points at different times to different audiences, all the while trying to convey truth. That is what the different types of writings in the Bible do, too.

In an effort to make the varying styles of the 73 books a little more understandable, I've broken them down into seven categories:

The Law
- Genesis
- Exodus
- Leviticus
- Numbers
- Deuteronomy

Historical (some Bibles list the last five as Narratives/ Novellas in their "own" section)
- Joshua
- Judges

- Ruth
- 1 Samuel
- 2 Samuel
- 1 Kings
- 2 Kings
- 1 Chronicles
- 2 Chronicles
- Ezra
- Nehemiah
- Tobit
- Judith
- Esther
- 1 Maccabees
- 2 Maccabees

Wisdom
- Job
- Psalms
- Proverbs
- Ecclesiastes
- Song of Songs
- Wisdom
- Sirach

The Prophets
- Isaiah
- Jeremiah
- Lamentations
- Baruch
- Ezekiel
- Daniel
- Hosea
- Joel
- Amos

- Obadiah
- Jonah
- Micah
- Nahum
- Habakkuk
- Zephaniah
- Haggai
- Zechariah
- Malachi

The Gospels
- Matthew
- Mark
- Luke
- John
- Acts of the Apostles (technically not a Gospel but a "sequel" to Luke's Gospel — it deserves a prominence all its own apart from the other New Testament letters and books)

The Epistles
- Romans
- 1 Corinthians
- 2 Corinthians
- Galatians
- Ephesians
- Philippians
- Colossians
- 1 Thessalonians
- 2 Thessalonians
- 1 Timothy
- 2 Timothy
- Titus
- Philemon

The (Other) New Testament Letters

- Hebrews
- James
- 1 Peter
- 2 Peter
- 1 John
- 2 John
- 3 John
- Jude
- Revelation (although people classify Revelation many different ways)

Hopefully this list will make it a little easier to spot consistencies and idiosyncrasies when reading different types of writing. Before you open a Biblical book, take a few minutes to look at the overview in this resource or read the introduction that (hopefully) precedes it in your own Bible. Remember, too, that the Catholic Church — given its long tradition and history — is invaluable at helping you navigate and read Scripture through its proper contextual lens.

Some stories are strictly historical, others completely symbolic. You'll come across many, however, that capture both senses and styles beautifully (divinely, I'd say). Take, for instance, the story of the man born blind in John chapter nine. This story is historically true — Jesus did, in fact, heal a blind man. This story is also very symbolic in that Jesus healed a man born blind (meaning original sin) and through the water of God (spit) and the ceremonial washing (in the pool of Siloam), the man was "reborn" in water (baptism) and light. This is a story not only of the historical and symbolic, but also of the prophetic and sacramental.

Taking time to read the introduction, as well as any footnotes your Bible might offer, is a great way to gain proper context and get even more out of your Bible.

PRAYING WITH SCRIPTURE

HOW TO START READING THE BIBLE

I meet tens of thousands of people a year at different events. Most of them are Catholic Christians who want to start reading the Bible but don't know where to start. So, if you've ever wanted to go deeper into God's Word but haven't known how to approach it, let me suggest a few tips (and allow you to learn from my mistakes).

Like anything else, if you want to build something — in this case, your knowledge and love for the Scriptures — you don't just grab a hammer and some nails and start pounding. There are things you can do to be more successful and ensure you don't jump in and then quit out of frustration or confusion.

We'll attack it on three levels: the tools, the blueprint, and the construction. By the end, you'll have ten steps to help you build your bodily temple into a Biblical fortress, able to resist anything the devil throws at you.

The Tools

Let's start with three things you should do before you start reading.

1. Pick a time, but not just any time. Commit to a daily time that you'll open God's Word but be sure it's an intelligent time. If you're really tired, for example, reading the Bible once you're in bed probably isn't the best idea. Pick a time when you're totally awake so you can give your full attention to the passage. Commit to ten minutes a day and work up to 20 minutes from there.

2. Pick a Bible you can understand. Get yourself a good, Catholic Bible so you'll have all 73 books. If you don't have one right now, it's OK. Don't let that stop you from reading. In reality, the best translation today is the one you already have.

It's important that your Bible is comfortable to read, light enough to take with you, durable enough to really use, and inexpensive enough that you don't feel bad writing or marking in it. I highly recommend the Life Teen Catholic Teen Bible for everyday use. It's durable and the additional 128 pages of content offer you even more of the practical insights you've found in this book. If you're looking for the "best" Catholic translation of the Bible, the Revised Standard Version Catholic Edition (RSVCE) is great as it is cross-referenced with the *Catechism of the Catholic Church*. You might also want to have a copy of the New American Bible (NAB), which is the translation the Life Teen Bible uses and is also the translation we hear at Mass. Regardless of which translation you choose, remember, your Bible is like a telescope — it's not meant to be looked at but, rather, looked through.

3. Have other books that help you understand *the BOOK*. There are some great resources out there designed to help you better understand the Bible, like those available through lifeteen.com and from other fine, Catholic publishers. It's also great to have the *Catechism of the Catholic Church* handy so you can use it as you read.

The Blueprint

Next, we'll cover three things you can do as you read.

1. Pray, and then pray some more. Before you open God's Word, ask the author of that Word — the Holy Spirit — to be present in a bold and fierce way. Quiet yourself, spend some time in silence, and hold the Bible in your hands as you pray. Ask God, through the power of His Spirit, to open your eyes, mind, and heart to His truth and thank Him for the gift of His Word. It doesn't have to be a long prayer but don't rush it — this is the most important step in your Bible study.

2. Have a plan. If you were planning on reading the Bible cover to cover, don't. The Bible isn't a novel; it wasn't designed to be read from Genesis straight through to Revelation. You must first learn the story of salvation history. You can access free video overviews and downloadable guides at biblegeek.com that will help you learn this story. Additionally, "The Great Adventure" Bible timeline series is a great resource for groups. There is a middle school version (Encounter), a teen version (T3), and a version for adults (TGA), all available at evangelization.com.

After you get the "big picture" of the Bible, you can focus on smaller portraits. I'd pick one book you are going to start with and make it your focus for a while. If you are starting from scratch, I'd suggest the Gospel of Mark. Mark's Gospel is the shortest and easiest to understand as you already know the main characters and plotline, as well as its personal significance and relevance to your faith walk. The Gospels are the hinge-pin to the entire

Bible — they're a great place to start and get into a reading "rhythm."

3. Get the background. If you do start in a Gospel, take time to learn about the author: Who was he? Who was he writing to? What are the basic themes of his Gospel account? Ask yourself what makes that specific account different than the other three. Similarly, don't just jump into a letter of St. Paul without knowing what is going on in the city to which he is writing. If you are reading a story from a prophet, know what was going on in his world at the time.

"Where do I learn these things?" you might ask. Read the introduction to the Gospel on the pages preceding it. Use one of your additional books or resources to help you. When you know what is going on with the author and the audience, the words will jump out at you in a much different way and give you far greater insight.

The Construction

Finally, let's hit four things you should remember while reading the Bible and beyond.

1. Less is more. Don't just open the Gospel and read until you get tired or "for 15 minutes" because that's what you committed to doing. Most Bibles break down the chapters into subchapters. If you begin with the Gospel of Mark, for instance, you shouldn't just start with verse 1 and continue through verse 45 (the end of the chapter). Instead, read verses 1-8 and spend 15 minutes meditating on them. Take verses 9-11 and reflect on them. The 45 verses of the first chapter should be broken down into about ten different studies alone. Studying Scripture is not like driving across country — it's not about how much distance you cover in a set amount of time, so roll the windows down, take everything in, and enjoy the ride.

2. Periods are there for a reason. The period at the end of a sentence is almost as much a gift as the words that precede it. Each little "dot" is an invitation to take a breath and reflect on what you just read. At each period, take a moment to envision the story that's unfolding. If you are reading about the baptism of Jesus (Mk 1:9-11), don't just say, "Hey cool, Jesus is getting baptized." Go deeper and insert yourself into the story. For instance, at Christ's baptism, where are you? Are you on the shore, on the mountain overlooking the scene, or in the water right next to Him? Is it hot out? Does the water smell bad? Is it noisy or peaceful? Let the story come alive.

3. Journal. As you read, write down any verses that confuse you or questions that arise. Don't allow yourself to get hung up on "tough verses." Scribble down the verse number with a question mark in a journal and keep moving. Later on, you can search the footnotes and other books or ask someone knowledgeable for more help. The journal isn't just for questions, though. You should also use it to write out reflections the verses stir within you. Write down images God gives you in your imagination and record key verses that stand out to you. God will reveal a great deal about who you are when you let Him.

4. Put the book down. Don't become a bookworm, who never takes their eyes off of the page. The Bible is the living Word (Jn 1:1-5, Heb 4:12). It lives and breathes well beyond the page that contains it. Share what you learn. Write out passages and hang them up in your room or locker. Send verses to your friends or put them on the fridge for your family to see. Just like the Eucharist, the Word should be taken, blessed, broken (down), and shared. The greatest gift you can give someone is to live a life that mirrors the Gospels, reflecting God in all you do. The second greatest gift is to invite others to peer into that mirror.

In Conclusion

OK, so that's a substantial start. Although there are several ways to begin reading Scripture, these are what I've found over the years to be the best, most realistic steps. Get the tools, pull together your blueprints, and start building your love for God's Word.

And don't just think that you have to "study" every time you open the Bible. It's great if you set aside 30-45 minutes every day to study, but that doesn't mean you can't flip through other books like the Psalms, Proverbs, Sirach, Wisdom, Ecclesiastes, or St. Paul's letters — you'll be blessed by all of them.

THINGS TO KEY INTO WHEN READING

Many people are too intimidated to read or study the Bible. Let's face it: The Bible can be a very intimidating book. It's big and heavy. It has hundreds of thousands of words, some of which are very difficult to pronounce. It has confusing sayings, hidden meanings, and cultural references that even Bible scholars argue about.

So how do we know what to look for when we are reading a passage but don't have the background information or education to help us figure it out? How can you "get something" out of a verse and "key into" the right parts of the text when reading a passage for the first time?

Here are a few suggestions:

1. Read in bite-sized chunks. Don't just read until your eyes get tired. Instead of reading an entire chapter at a time, for instance, read a chapter in several pieces. Read and pray through one subchapter at a time.

2. Get the big picture of the passage. As you read, ask yourself the basic "big picture" questions of who, what, when, where, why, and how. The introduction to each book will help you answer these questions.

Some specific questions to ask yourself are:

• Who is involved in this story I'm reading? Who is speaking? To whom is he/she speaking?

- What is being said? What is the main point being made? (This might take reading the footnotes and asking additional questions.)

- When is this event taking place? At what point in history is this being said? Where am I in the Bible, right now?

- Where is this taking place? Are the people listening friends or enemies? Are they receptive or uninterested in the message?

- Why is this being said? Why was this important for the people to hear at that specific moment? Why is it important for me to hear now?

- How does this apply to my life today? How does this truth challenge me to live differently?

Now, you might not know the answer to each of these questions immediately, but the more information you have when it comes to the big picture, the less likely you are to get confused or caught up in the little details.

3. Get the smaller picture, too. Once you get the "lay of the land" and have a feel for the who, what, when, where, why, and how of a passage, it's time to read over the section again and look for details. These details are clues that can help you uncover the buried treasure of wisdom that might not be visible at first.

- *Look for details.* For example, does the passage mention the time of day, what the scene looked like, or anything else that gives you a mental picture?

Check out the details in the following passages from Mark's Gospel: 1:32-33, 4:35-38, 5.2 5, 6:39-40. Look for details such as these to help you better understand the passage.

* *Look for emotions.* Were the people angry, confused, overjoyed, afraid, or expressing any other emotion? Again, read through these passages from Mark's Gospel and note the details he gives about peoples' emotional responses: 1:40, 3:1-5, 10:13-15, 14:33-34.

* *Look for numbers.* Numbers carry heavy symbolic meaning in the Bible and are used to convey certain truths and make a point when necessary. You'll notice certain numbers — like 3, 7, 12, and 40 — are used frequently. You'll notice other numbers — like 666 or 144,000 — are often times taken out of context and ascribed meanings that were never intended by the original writer. It's helpful to check the footnotes and other trusted Catholic resources rather than getting carried away by false teachings, ridiculous websites, or our own misconceptions. Pay attention to numbers and realize they are there for a purpose, even if the purpose is not obvious at first.

Other Specifics to Watch For

Pay attention to names, locations, colors, and verb choice. These details are important because they lend credibility to a passage, remind us of another passage, or communicate the passion and depth of a scene.

Other Sections that Will Help You

The more time you can take to read the explanatory sections — the introductions to the different books, the footnotes, the *Catechism of the Catholic Church*, and other reliable books and commentaries — the better equipped you will be to understand the little details and not get sidetracked when reading a story.

When it comes to reading Scripture, the best advice is always this: Take your time; it's not a sprint, it's a marathon. And remember, it's a fun run. If it's not fun, you might be running too fast. The idea is to put yourself "into" the story as you go. It's as if you're running alongside the characters, not watching them from the sidelines.

AN INTRODUCTION TO *LECTIO DIVINA*

So how do you put yourself "into" the story when you're reading the Bible, anyway?

One of the best parts about being Catholic is that we have many different forms of prayer that help us encounter God more deeply. For more than a thousand years, Catholics have been praying the Scriptures with an approach called "*lectio divina*," which means "sacred/divine reading" in Latin.

Have you ever had a conversation with a friend that you find yourself thinking about over and over again? Maybe you play the conversation back in your head a thousand times, remembering what you said, what you wish you hadn't said, and what you feel you should have said. You probably even remember the less important details: where you were, how hot or cold it was, what music or movie was playing in the background, and what you were wearing at the time. The more you think about it, break it down, and analyze it, the more all of those other details come to life. *Lectio divina* is similar to this; it's a slow and intentional way of praying the Bible while talking to and spending time with God. It's designed to help the story come to life in your mind and heart and (re) capture your soul. It's designed to help you become more and more contemplative.

Lectio divina is as easy as four steps. Historically, these four steps are known as:

1. Lectio (Reading)
2. Meditatio (Meditation)
3. Oratio (Praying/Speaking)
4. Contemplatio (Contemplation)

Since you probably don't know Latin, it might be easier to remember the steps as:

1. Read
2. Reflect
3. Respond
4. Rest

Whichever list you choose to remember, the steps are simple to follow. But before we dive into some passages, it's vital that you understand a few more things.

First, it's important to identify what *lectio divina* is not. When we pray through Scripture using *lectio divina*, we are not doing a formal "Scripture study." It can be helpful to know the background of what we are reading, what some of the words mean, and who the characters are, but we aren't going to take a lot of time to look at footnotes or pull out a Biblical concordance to look up the history of a location or etymology of a particular word. Again, those aren't bad things — they are important and necessary parts of learning the Bible — they just aren't things we do when we pray *lectio divina*.

Second, *lectio divina* is not about getting some Earth-shattering revelation. Don't enter in thinking that walls are going to shake and God is going to speak to you, answering all of your questions and solving all of your problems. Sometimes the greatest gifts from God are the simplest ones — a gentle nudge in the right direction, a reaffirmation of something you know but seem to forget, or a word of encouragement. When we enter into *lectio divina* (and really any prayer) with an agenda of what we want or "expect" to hear, it rarely turns out well. Approach prayer with an open mind and heart to receive whatever God wants to give you. It will be exactly what you need.

Finally, *lectio divina* is not hard to learn, but it does take practice. It alternates between being "active" (reading and speaking) and "passive" (meditating, contemplating, and receiving). In our daily life, we are accustomed to "doing" rather than "being," so we are generally more comfortable with active prayer than with passive prayer. Don't get discouraged if you feel like your prayer isn't going well or if you are having a hard time "getting it." Prayer involves practice and the more you pray, the better you will become.

Now, what exactly do you "do" in each step?

The best way to start praying *lectio divina* is to grab your Bible, find a quiet space where you won't be disturbed, and put your phone on airplane mode. Before opening your Bible, spend a few moments in serious and silent prayer. Focus on your breathing. Ask the Holy Spirit to enlighten your mind and open your heart. Now, let's begin.

1. Read (Lectio)

Select a passage or use one from the list on pages 66-67. Read it slowly, all the way through. As you read the passage, envision the scene. Watch for adjectives and pay attention to details. Really "enter into" the moment. If you're reading a Gospel passage, lock eyes with Jesus as you encounter Him in the story.

Take a breath. Inhale and exhale deeply. Put distractions out of your mind and slowly read the passage a second time. Now, read it a third time. This isn't speed-reading. Allow the words to roll over you. As you read, be aware of any word or phrase that stands out to you. What resonates with you or "jumps off the page"? It is likely that God wants to use this particular word, phrase, or image to speak to you. Hold onto it, you'll need it for the next part of the prayer.

2. Reflect (Meditatio)

Now, what is the main "point" of the passage you just read? What words jumped out at you? What words "spoke" to your heart? Were they comforting? Did the passage make you uncomfortable, and, if so, why? If nothing jumps out at you, read the passage once more and ask how it applies to life in the 21st century. If you don't think it applies to you, look harder. This is where you really "chew" on the words of the passage and ask yourself questions. Other thoughts, images, words, or distractions may enter into your prayer. It's all right — the worst thing you can do is try to ignore them. Instead, acknowledge the distraction (but don't follow it) and return to your meditation. There is no time limit for how long this step should take, but for now, set a timer for five minutes and work to increase it one minute each day until you hit ten minutes. As you practice *lectio divina* more, you will start to feel when you need to move on.

3. Respond (Oratio)

Step three is where you and God speak to one another. If you're praying *lectio divina* alone, this is where you can ask God questions, but it's important to listen as well and not just speak. Bring anything that stood out to you in step two to Him, now. Spend some time in silence and let God speak to your heart. Remember, this is about responding to God not only with your words, but with your heart.

If you're praying *lectio divina* with a group, this is where you can discuss what the passage meant to you personally, what you liked, and what challenged you. Either way, it's important to listen to God as He speaks to your heart or through other people. This is also a great place to take out your journal and start writing. Be sure to note the Scripture passage you are reflecting upon and the word or phrase that stood out to you. These journals can be a powerful witness to the ways God has moved — and is moving — in your life.

4. Rest (Contemplatio)

During this final step, you simply "rest." This step might be difficult for you. If you're the type of person (like I am) who frequently reaches for your phone when things get "too quiet," this part will definitely challenge you. That's a good thing — it shows that you're taking it seriously and that the Holy Spirit is growing you spiritually. Say no to the temptation and try not to let yourself get distracted.

This is where you really become a child of God, again. Resting in your heavenly Father's presence is like crawling up onto His lap and letting Him hold you. It might take some "practice" at first to just sit with God and let Him love you. It might even make you uncomfortable to be so vulnerable, trusting God does love you and wants to draw near to you, but let Him. Picture God staring into your eyes. Imagine Him telling you how proud He is of you and the person you are becoming. Let Him remind you how much you mean to Him and all He desires for you.

Allow thoughts to come and go in this fourth step and simply be mindful that you are in God's presence. It's that simple — and also that difficult. Ultimately, contemplation is about sitting with all that was given through the Word of God and allowing it to sink in. It's as though you've slowed down to realize and recognize different things (dots) in the first three steps and now, in this fourth step, God wants to connect the dots for you, but only if you allow Him to do so.

PUTTING *LECTIO DIVINA* INTO PRACTICE

Now, let's put these steps into practice.

Choose a passage and dedicate 20 minutes to praying with it. Set a timer or have a watch nearby to keep track of the time. Allot each movement about five minutes. Be mindful of where you struggle or feel tempted to cut corners and give those areas extra attention and effort.

Below are a few suggested readings with rich imagery that you can use as a jumpstart:

Mark 1:9-11 – A lot happens in three short verses. Take your time to really enter into the scene. What did it look and smell like? Is God proclaiming a truth only about Jesus or about you, his son/daughter, too?

John 2:1-12 – What do you learn about God in this scene? What about the role of His mother? Does she say anything that strikes you?

Luke 8:49-56 – What is Jesus trying to teach you in this scene? What is His response to doubters? Who does Jesus allow to enter and witness the miracle? Why?

Matthew 14:22-33 – Why didn't the apostles display greater trust before Jesus showed up? Have you ever felt like that? What can you learn from this scene with Peter? How can this story still bring hope, today?

John 13:1-9 – What does Jesus' example teach you? Why is this a vital lesson for the apostles to learn before they begin their ministry? Where are you called to do as Jesus has done here?

Luke 23:33-43 – Note the two different quotes and approaches of the thieves. When you experience suffering in your own life, which thieves' "prayer" most resembles your own? Why? What can you learn from this episode of suffering?

1 Kings 19:9-13 – This is our opening story. There is a lot to pray through, here, especially if you are thinking about how God's voice is present in your life.

Psalm 139:1-13 – This psalm focuses on how God knows us perfectly and is great to pray through if you are feeling distant from God.

Romans 12:9-18 – Saint Paul writes a list of what an ideal disciple looks like. It is convicting by itself but, through prayer, becomes even more challenging as the Holy Spirit identities specific areas we need to work through.

1 John 3:1-3 – John's letters are quick reads, but this short passage packs a punch as it quickly identifies who we are and who we belong to.

Those are just a few passages to get you started, but there are many more. Look for them, remember them, and start your journal. Once the Word transforms your life, you will find yourself coming back to *lectio divina* again and again, and your life will never be the same.

UNDERSTANDING
SCRIPTURE

THE STORY OF SALVATION IN
THE OLD TESTAMENT

Some modern Christians believe you don't really need the Old Testament anymore, mistakenly thinking the New Testament is superior or somehow renders its predecessor "outdated."

Nothing could be further from the truth.

While Jesus is absolutely the center of the Bible, simply focusing on the New Testament is dangerously short-sighted. Jesus is the key that unlocks everything, but without an understanding of the Old Testament — its prophecy, promise, fulfillment, covenants, and "plan" for salvation and the coming Messiah — you cannot fully understand or appreciate Jesus Christ and His mission. The Old Testament is like an arrow that points forward to Jesus. The New Testament points back and "unpacks" the Old Testament, demonstrating that all of God's promises come to life and take flesh in Christ. The grace and power *concealed* in the pages of the Old Testament are *revealed* in the identity and actions of Jesus in the New Testament (CCC 129).

Beginning in **Genesis** we see that God — who is love — creates everything to demonstrate love, most especially when he creates the male and female, in his own identity, to mirror and reflect the nature of self-giving love. As the family grows, so does the potential to love or to sin. When the fall happens in the garden and sin enters the story in **Genesis 3**, we immediately hear God promise us a redeemer (Messiah) who will restore our relationship. In the pages that follow, we see God's family grow with characters like Noah (**Genesis 6**), Abraham (**Genesis 11**), and their families. God enters into sacred relationships — covenants — with these characters. As their families grow, so does sin. We begin to see a "cycle" of our humanity and personalities: we follow God, we turn away from God, God proactively reaches out to restore the relationship through sacrifice and penance.

We see God treat the nation of Israel like His own child, guiding and instructing the people through good times and bad. By the time Moses comes onto the scene in **Exodus**, God's children are enslaved in Egypt. We see the burning bush (**Exodus 3**) and the warnings of the ten plagues (**Exodus 7-12**) before the great escape through the Red Sea and the giving of the Ten Commandments in **Exodus 20**. Then, because of their lack of faith, God is forced to correct and instruct the Israelites, again. Reading through **Numbers**, **Leviticus**, and **Deuteronomy** we hear the early lessons for God's wandering people, His first priests, and the young nation headed to their Promised Land.

These books — **Genesis**, **Exodus**, **Leviticus**, **Numbers**, and **Deuteronomy** — are known as the "Torah" or the "Pentateuch." They are the first five books of the Old Testament, the "Books of the Law." Traditionally, Moses has been identified as their author.

Genesis means "beginning" and tells about how God created everything from nothing. In addition to the story of Adam and Eve, you'll read about Cain and Abel, Noah and the flood, the Tower of Babel, Abraham and Sarah and their son, Isaac, as well as other famous figures like Jacob and Joseph and his jealous brothers.

Exodus means "going out" and tells the story of Moses leading the children of God (Israel) out of slavery in Egypt. It tells about their 40-year journey through the desert on their way to the Promised Land.

Leviticus is a handbook for the early priests — the Levites — who came from the tribe of Levi. It talks about religious and liturgical laws (how to worship, prepare for worship, offer sacrifice, etc.) and reminds them of the need to be holy and intentional in how they worship God.

Numbers tells the story of Israel's 40-year wandering through the desert. God's original plan to take His children straight to the Promised Land gets sidetracked because of disobedience and faithlessness. The decades of journey reveal several lessons about trusting God and living through hardship, reminding us that sin never pays.

Deuteronomy means "second law" and while it repeats the Ten Commandments, it also adds new ("second") laws about the way the Israelites should live to enjoy holy lives and families. It contains practical advice and wisdom as well as several prophecies about what is to come.

It's at this point in the story that we shift into what are called the **historical books**. As you may have already guessed, they are books that recount the history of the nation of Israel.

We pick up the action in **Joshua**, who rises as the new leader following the death of Moses. In this book, we see God's people overthrow Jericho and take their rightful place in the Promised Land after years of struggle. Next, as the Israelites finally become a true nation (and not just enslaved tribes living in community), we read **Judges** to see their early system of authority and leadership. When they begin calling out for a king like all of the surrounding countries and empires, God warns them of the negatives that come with aristocracy. God wanted to be their sole leader and king, but the people "knew better." We read about how that goes —all the ups and downs that come with people fighting for power — in **1 and 2 Samuel** and **1 and 2 Kings** (and its counterpart, the not-so-exciting **1 and 2 Chronicles**).

The Kingdom splits in half, falls into ruin, is taken into slavery, and is ultimately left in ashes. Fast forwarding, we see God's children taken off into slavery (again) and, finally, returning to rebuild God's Kingdom on Earth. In the books of **Ezra** and **Nehemiah**, we hear stories recounting the hardships and victories of rebuilding the Temple, the city walls, and the God-loving culture that once existed. It's during these centuries that we are also introduced to heroes and heroines like **Ruth**, **Tobit**, **Judith**, and **Esther**. Following the period of the prophets (which you'll hear about later) and the time of rebuilding the world, power shifts from Babylon to Persia to Greece. It's at that time — under Greek rule — that the Jews are asked and forced to live as Greeks and worship false gods. In **1 and 2 Maccabees**, we read about a brave band of Israelites who, though outnumbered and out-trained, take on the mighty Greek armies and defeat them for the glory of God.

Here's a brief breakdown of each of the **historical books**:

Joshua was Robin to Moses' Batman. When the famous prophet died, Joshua led the children of Israel through their conquest of Canaan (the Promised Land). The book is filled with wars, fighting, fidelity, and faithlessness that reveal who loves God and who merely says they do.

Judges traces the story of the children of Israel after Joshua's death. The family was still "divided" into their own tribes and without a clear leader, they fell into disagreements and strife. After repeatedly disobeying God and getting overthrown in small wars with enemies, God raises up a series of different "judges" to lead them back to Him.

Ruth was a non-Israelite convert to the faith. Her deep love for family and God unveiled her strength and faithfulness in the face of incredible personal adversity. Ruth goes on to be the great-grandmother of King David and an ancestor of Jesus, Himself.

1 and 2 Samuel tell the stories of the first kings of Israel. Beginning with a king named Saul, we see what happens when you make God the priority and when you try to make yourself "god" in the eyes of all. Following Saul, the great King David takes the reigns and although he loves God, he also sins. These books demonstrate the rise and fall of kings and the dangers of earthly power.

1 and 2 Kings pick up the story of the kings of Israel who followed the great King David. Beginning with his son,

Solomon, we read of the construction of the Temple in Jerusalem, Solomon's fall from grace, and the series of kings (mostly bad) who succeeded him in the decades to come. The main event we read about is the Kingdom of Israel splitting in two, despite God's repeated warnings through His prophets. The northern kingdom would now be called "Israel" and would settle in the north, while the southern kingdom would remain centered around Jerusalem in the south and be called "Judah."

1 and 2 Chronicles recount the same history contained in 1 and 2 Samuel and 1 and 2 Kings but from a *religious* or *liturgical* point of view. In other words, 1 and 2 Chronicles spend more time talking about the building of the Temple and the spiritual aspects of the kingdoms (especially the southern kingdom, Judah, which was generally more faithful).

Ezra describes the events that occur when the Jews are allowed to return to Jerusalem after it was destroyed and their exile in Babylon was over. It recounts their efforts to rebuild the Temple and reestablish proper worship.

Nehemiah also describes the events surrounding the Jewish return to Jerusalem and their desire to live in obedience to the law of Moses.

Tobit is a story with a "happy ending." Even though times are tough, Tobit remains faithful to God and His law. Tobiah (Tobit's son) follows in his father's righteous footsteps and rejects sin as he begins his own family. The book shows how God blesses and protects those who follow Him in true love and purity.

Judith recounts one brave, faithful woman's efforts to save Israel. Her trust in God is the key and reason for her success. This book shows how important it is for us to trust in God's love and mercy, even when we don't understand what He's up to.

Esther recounts the story of another brave Israelite woman who becomes the queen of Persia. As beautiful as she is courageous, Esther risks her life to prevent an evil murderer from harming God's people.

1 and 2 Maccabees describe what happens after the time of the prophets until Jesus comes onto the scene in the New Testament. These amazing books recount the story of a family (the Maccabees) who led a revolt against the Greek rulers when they tried to impose worship of false gods on the Jewish people. They act as the "bridge" between Old and New Testaments and are not included in Protestant (non-Catholic) Bibles.

What you've read so far is a narrative re-telling of the entire Old Testament. While these stories were playing out chronologically, God continued to speak to His people through wisdom and prophecy, which we will deal with separately.

The **wisdom books** of the Bible are really fun to read. Filled with practical wisdom, still useful today, they speak to life's situations from birth to death and virtually everything in between. They don't recount Israel's history and aren't really prophetic in their tone, either. In the wisdom books, you'll read songs (**Psalms**), practical insights (**Proverbs** and **Sirach**), poetry (**Song of Songs**), philosophy (**Ecclesiastes**), and a lot more.

Each of these books answers questions about how God moves and thinks as well as how we respond to Him and one another. In short, the wisdom books talk about the beauty, majesty, mercy, and awesome power of God and how we should let them affect our lives.

Job addresses one of life's oldest questions: Why does God let bad things happen to good people? Job loses everything, is surrounded by friends who encourage him to quit on God, and actually converses with God about why life has suffering. It's an invitation to think bigger and trust in God, even when we can't "figure out" his ultimate plan.

Psalms is the longest book in the Bible. It is a collection of religious prayers, poems, and songs, many of which were written by King David. These are read (or sung) at every Mass.

Proverbs contains many insightful, wise sayings and teachings, many of which are believed to have come from King Solomon. This book is a practical guide to good and proper living.

Ecclesiastes is basically a book on philosophy. It analyzes the meaning — or lack thereof — of life and, in particular, a life without God. It discusses love of money and possessions, the emptiness and fleeting nature of beauty and material possessions and some relationships, all the while asking, "What in life is truly satisfying?"

Song of Songs (Song of Solomon) is poetry — more of a "love poem," actually — written in the form of a dialogue between a young bride and her new husband. This book is supposed to be a reflection of the love of Christ (the groom) for His bride (the Church).

Wisdom of Solomon is a long poem about the beauty, value, and importance of wisdom in and to our daily lives.

Sirach (Ben Sira) is an honest look at the challenges that arise when someone tries to live a godly life in an ungodly world. Filled with timeless wisdom that is still applicable in everyday life and relationships, it offers advice for those seeking to be to be faithful to truth and virtue in a society that wants to reject them.

As mentioned prior to the last section, during the period where Israel's kings were good and not-so-good, listening to God and ignoring Him completely, God loved His people enough to send living, breathing "warnings" in the prophets. We hear about the adventures of famous prophets like Elijah and Elisha in the books of Kings. There are actually over a dozen books written (or attributed to) prophets, including major prophets like **Isaiah**, **Jeremiah**, and **Ezekiel** and minor prophets like **Micah** and **Hosea**. When we think of prophets, we tend to think of old, crazy guys with long beards who lived in a cave somewhere in the desert and made predictions about the future. But the truth is that prophets are messengers from God, sent to speak His words to His people. They would often warn the people that tragedies and disasters would strike if they continued to disobey God and His commands. They weren't "gloomy" all the time; when disasters or tragedies did occur, God often spoke words of comfort and hope through these mouthpieces. Not only did they warn of things to come "in their time," but they also spoke of the coming one — the Messiah — in prophecies, details, and predictions they shared *literally hundreds of years* before Jesus' birth in Bethlehem.

Here's a brief rundown of the main themes and topics covered in the **prophetic books**:

Isaiah is the most famous and significant prophetic book, quoted by Jesus more than any other. It discusses the coming of Christ, warnings for those who do not turn from sin, the fall of the Kingdom of Judah, and God's forgiveness and promise of redemption.

Jeremiah was a holy, young man given a hard message to spread. He tells Judah (the southern kingdom) that they will be destroyed if they do not repent and turn from their sinful ways. Readers are given a very personal and intimate glimpse into the prophet Jeremiah's life in this book.

Lamentations is like listening to Blues music. The book is a collection of poems written during and after the destruction of Jerusalem (when the Kingdom of Judah fell to the Babylonians).

Baruch shares a message he receives from God that there will be a new and everlasting covenant between God and the people of Israel. It is "good news" that comes during hard times.

Ezekiel contains many mysterious symbols and images describing the judgment that will fall upon Israel. It also speaks of great hope: God will resurrect the "dead bones" of Israel and breathe new life into them, again,

Daniel tells the story of a holy, young prophet who was captured by the Babylonians and taken into exile. Daniel is known for his ability to interpret dreams, his fidelity to prayer, and the famous story of surviving the lion's den.

Hosea describes the unhappy marriage between a man and his wife. The wife is unfaithful to her husband, but he takes her back. The story demonstrates the way in which God always takes back His people even when they are unfaithful to Him.

Joel warns the Kingdom of Judah about the coming capture and judgment, but speaks with hope for the future, promising that God's Spirit will be poured out upon all people.

Amos was pretty disliked by the people of Israel. He spoke about the coming judgment they would face if they continued in their disobedience. Although he issued a stern warning, Amos also spoke with hope about the day when all of Israel would be reunited.

Obadiah foretells the unpleasant future of Judah's great enemy, Edom. The shortest book in the Old Testament, Obadiah demonstrates how justice ultimately prevails against those who disrespect and abuse the Lord's people.

Jonah recounts the famous story about the prophet who disobeyed God and (originally) refused to preach

His message to the people of Nineveh. While most well-known for the "whale story," this book is a tremendous lesson about God's mercy and unconditional love not only toward His "enemies" but those supposedly close to Him as well.

Micah speaks of the judgment that will come to those who do evil — especially "in the Lord's name" — but also of the great hope that will come when the Savior is born in a little village known as Bethlehem (a prophecy which occurs five to six centuries before the birth of Christ).

Nahum prophesies about the end of Nineveh, which was the central city in the evil Assyrian Empire. His "bad news" was considered good news by many.

Habakkuk also speaks of the judgment that will come upon those who do evil and offers comfort to those who live faith-filled lives, following the Lord and keeping His commandments.

Zephaniah is different than the other prophets. He doesn't just speak about the judgment of God on Israel and Judah; he widens the scope to speak about the judgment of God against the entire world. Even though it is rather stern, Zephaniah is also filled with hope for the future.

Haggai was one of the leaders in the efforts to rebuild the Temple after its destruction. He was angered because some people were content to live comfortably when God's house was in shambles.

Zechariah was a peer and contemporary of Haggai and also supported the rebuilding of the Temple. He devoted his time and energy to the Temple because it was the place where God's people worshipped Him and received strength and guidance.

Malachi warns the returning Jews that external religious offerings and sacrifices are not enough — God desires righteous living as proof of our love and faith.

THE MOST IMPORTANT BOOK(S) IN THE WORLD: THE GOSPEL(S)

As mentioned earlier, there are many different types of writing and books within this big, holy book we call the Bible. Out of the 73 books, however, four books stand alone: The Gospels. All of the books in the Bible are inspired by God and are free from error, but the four Gospels are unique and supremely important.

In the Gospels, we are not only given prophecies about the coming Messiah (Jesus), we receive the Messiah Himself in flesh and blood. We see His face and hear His voice. We watch Him interact with all of humanity — sinners and saints, holy and unholy, and everyone in between. We encounter God in an entirely new way, and everything we read about in the Old Testament is now fulfilled.

Jesus is the one all have been waiting for, the one who died for us so we would not have to do so. It is with the Gospel, as the foundation of your life, that you will come to know the love of God and learn how to share that love with your friends, family, and, ultimately, a world desperately in need of it. Everything you desire to know, everything you wonder about God, every fear and every hope, every pain and every joy collide and find meaning within the Gospel of Jesus Christ.

Pope St. John Paul II put it this way: *"It is Jesus that you seek when you dream of happiness; he is waiting for you when nothing else you find satisfies you... it is Jesus who stirs in you the desire to do something great with your lives."* [2]

The same Holy Spirit who inspired these words from St. John Paul II moved through the pens of the four Gospel writers: Matthew, Mark, Luke, and John. Now, to be clear, the Christ you encounter on the pages of their Gospels is not a "nice Jesus" here to make everyone happy. Far from it, actually. When you encounter Jesus in the Gospels, you see four portraits of the one, true God who became man in Christ Jesus.

Each Gospel writer has a certain and distinct "audience" they are writing for, which explains why they go to such lengths to explain certain details and not others. You'll find many similarities between Matthew, Mark, and Luke, for instance, which is why they are called the *synoptic Gospels* (synoptic means "like visioned"). Most Biblical scholars believe Mark's Gospel came first, and that Matthew and Luke borrowed from and used Mark's Gospel as a framework and outline. Others contest that Matthew's Gospel came first. Regardless, it's obvious the three have several parallels in structure but also offer many unique stories and perspectives on the life and ministry of Jesus Christ. You'll notice, too, that John's Gospel is drastically different in structure, tone, and goal. These small differences between the Gospels should make us feel even more confident in their authenticity for if they were all the exact same, we would wonder if it was really four different writers or just one. The differences in details between the Gospels, in this way, actually serve to bolster our confidence in their historic reality and truth.

Use the sections that follow to help you better understand the differences, but also the likenesses, in the Gospel portraits. Go back to the Gospels repeatedly and you will notice something amazing. While the words and truths don't change over time, *they will change you,* and over time you will begin to experience a real hunger for them.

GOSPEL SNAPSHOTS

The Gospel of Matthew

One of the original Twelve Apostles, Matthew (also called "Levi") was a tax collector working at a customs post when Christ invited him to follow (Mark 2:14).

Key Themes for Understanding Matthew's Gospel:

• Jesus was the Messiah they had been waiting thousands of years for to come and save them.

• Jesus did not come to abolish the law of Moses but to fulfill it (Matthew 5:17). He did not render the Old Testament and its covenants null and void, but unpacked, clarified, and explained them by His life, death, and Resurrection.

• Jesus came to begin His Kingdom, one we are invited to enter by His grace.

• Jesus institutes a Church on Earth to teach His truth and administer His sacraments, to baptize and initiate everyone on Earth with a universal message of mercy and love.

• The central theme is that Christ, the Messiah and king, came to establish a Church.

The Gospel of Mark

We know little about the author of this Gospel except that his birth name was probably John Mark (John, his

Jewish name, and Mark, his Roman name) and that he was a traveling companion of both Peter and Paul (2 Timothy 4:11, Colossians 4:10).

<u>Key Themes for Understanding Mark's Gospel:</u>

- Jesus was a man of action, of promises not just premises.

- Jesus was powerful because He was a servant, not a conqueror.

- Jesus is our mediator (our "go between") to God. He provides us with authority to teach and preach.

- As apostles and eyewitness, began dying off, this Gospel was written to reaffirm to people the centrality and primacy of Jesus Christ within the early Church.

- The central theme is action and service more than teachings.

The Gospel of Luke

Luke was not a Jew, but rather, a Gentile convert to Christianity. We also know he was a physician by profession and as such, was quite methodical in his approach to writing both the Gospel and Acts of the Apostles. Finally, we know he was a traveling companion to Paul for at least a while (Philippians 1:24, 2 Timothy 4:11, Colossians 4:14).

Key Themes for Understanding Luke's Gospel:

- It emphasizes Jesus' compassion for the poor, needy, sick, and helpless while putting a focus on the need for humility and the power of prayer.

- It reveals God's glory, mercy, and the desire/ willingness to heal us all spiritually and physically.

- Luke focuses on the power of the Holy Spirit, God's grace, and our ultimate salvation.

- It uplifts the dignity of all women in a time and culture that often did not do so; it offers an especially detailed and poignant portrait of the Blessed Virgin Mary.

- The central theme is freedom, liberation, and healing.

The Gospel of John

John is believed to be the writer of the final Gospel, as well as of the three letters which bear his name and the Book of Revelation. He was the younger brother of James and together, these "sons of Zebedee" worked as fishing partners of Simon Peter and Andrew. John is also called the "beloved disciple" and was entrusted with Mary's care following Jesus' Crucifixion (John 13:23, 19:26). He was most likely the youngest of the apostles and lived the longest of the 12. He was the only apostle not to die a martyr. The writing of the Gospel has extraordinary detail that had to come from an eyewitness.

<u>Key Themes for Understanding John's Gospel:</u>

- John wasn't writing "another biography" of Jesus to add to the others; he assumes readers are familiar with the other Gospels.

- It shows that Jesus of Nazareth is (prophesied) the Son of God.

- It explains to Christians how to root their religious beliefs and practices in Jesus (through the sacraments) and how, by doing so, faith will lead to eternal life.

- It explains why Jesus came, who He is, what He did, and how it relates to the life of the early Church followers.

- The central theme is the identity of Jesus and what that means to living our faith sacramentally.

Now that we've skimmed the Gospel waters in our overviews, let's pause on each of the four and do a little deep-sea diving to see what important themes and insights lie beneath the surface.

UNDERSTANDING MATTHEW:
AN OVERVIEW WITH EXERCISES

Over the years, I've noticed that my wife and I tell stories differently depending on the person we are speaking with and the subject matter of the conversation. When I communicate, it is often in an effort to exchange information. When my wife communicates, it is more often an opportunity to share a feeling, experience, or emotion. Conversationally speaking, I opt for brevity while my wife offers depth. This is not to sound derogatory in any way, only to demonstrate that who we are speaking to and their interests greatly influence our message, tone, and approach. It is this type of "difference" that sets Matthew's Gospel apart from his synoptic friends Mark and Luke and offers a stunning literary difference from John.

Matthew was a Jew writing to Jews about a Jew who claimed to be the King of the Jews, who some of the leading Jews then hatched a plot to have killed. That being said, there are a lot of references to Jewish customs, culture, idioms, and history that would have made perfect sense to a Jew from that age but may be lost on non-Jewish readers. It's for this reason you'll see a heavy emphasis on and use of the Old Testament (Hebrew Scriptures) throughout Matthew's Gospel. Matthew quotes the prophet Isaiah, for instance, throughout his Gospel and refers to Moses more than anyone else as these two figures were the preeminent prophets to the Jewish people, considered greater than all the rest. If you're new to reading Scripture and want to get the most out of this first Gospel account, it is important to have a good study Bible with footnotes and expansive explanation sections.

The first 18 verses of Matthew's Gospel offer us an intriguing family history, called a genealogy. Since Matthew is writing to Jews, he traces the bloodline of Jesus all the way back to Abraham, the great patriarch and forefather of faith. To modern minds, this type of opening might be considered boring and "off-putting" — not exactly a page turner that inspires a soul to keep reading. One might even wonder what this has to do with life today or what purpose it could possibly serve to know Jesus' family tree. The most common tendency is to merely skip the genealogy and pick up with the birth of Jesus in verse 18. Doing so, however, is short-sighted and misses not only the importance of the Old Testament and Christ's ancestry but also, the purpose and audience of Matthew's Gospel, in general.

You might be surprised by how much you have in common with Jesus. He wasn't born into a "perfect" family. Many of the ancestors in Jesus' line lived far less than saintly lives, a reality that should give us great hope. Many know how Jesus' earthly story "ends," with His Ascension and the birth of the Church. Now, go back and see how it all began. Pay attention to names you recognize and look up those you don't. You'll notice, too, there are five women mentioned in the family tree, all of whom are very important additions to a list that customarily would have included only the names of men.

In Matthew's Gospel, we hear not of the shepherds but the magi visiting the newborn king, fulfilling the prophecies of old (Numbers 24:17, Micah 5:2, Isaiah 60:6). We are given the extended form of the "most famous sermon ever preached," the Sermon on the Mount (Matthew 5-7). Many people think the sermon is merely the Beatitudes or, worse yet, that the Beatitudes are all about "being a nice person." But if you read Christ's sermon through, you'll soon see that perhaps nowhere else in the Gospel does Jesus say more about the reality of heaven and hell, sin and judgment, and God's justice. Christ is emphatic, pointed, precise, practical, and merciful at every turn.

It is only in Matthew that we are given the amazing conversation between Jesus and Simon as the penitent fisherman becomes our first (papal) shepherd, Peter (Matthew 16). Jesus Christ reveals not only His plan to build a Church, but also how He will build it and where His plan of salvation, brought to life through the Church, will take us.

Without the Holy Spirit breathing through Matthew's pen, we would not have the account of Peter walking on water (14:28-33), the dream of Pilate's wife (27:19), the appearance to the 11 (28:16-20), or Judas' remorse and suicide (27:3-10). Several parables, too, are unique to Matthew, including the field sown with weeds (13:24-30), the pearl of great price (13:44-46), the unforgiving servant (18:23-35), the laborers in the vineyard (20:1-16), and the foolish virgins (25:1-13). Matthew's Gospel also places a greater emphasis on money than the other three Gospels, which is not surprising given his previous career as a tax collector.

Now we are going to jump into several passages from Matthew to get a feel for his writing style and go deeper into the words of Jesus, Himself.

Exercise One: Jesus Calls Us to Follow Him Today

Matthew 4:18-22

Questions

1. What did Jesus mean when He said, "I will make you fishers of men"?
2. When do you think is the best time to start following Jesus?
3. What are you willing to give up in order to follow Jesus?

Reflection

Jesus isn't just calling the disciples in the story, He is calling all of us to follow Him. The disciples were some of the most unlikely of choices and so are we. None of us are perfect, but none of the disciples were either. Drop your nets and follow Jesus. He has an awesome plan for your life. Think about the people or activities you put before Jesus: school, friends, sports, etc. Now make a conscious effort to rearrange these in order to put God first.

Prayer

Jesus, help me hear your voice. Help me see that above everything in my life, I am your disciple. I will follow you Lord, wherever you lead me. I will depend on your wisdom, not mine, to guide me. Give me words of faith to tell my friends about you and your awesome love. May you shine in all that I do so they would know you are the reason for my joy. Amen.

Exercise Two: Jesus Calls Us to Love Our Enemies

Matthew 5:43-48

Questions

1. How does one love an enemy?
2. Give an example of someone who has shown love to an enemy.
3. Is it possible to be "perfect, just as your heavenly Father is perfect"? What do you think Jesus meant by that statement?

Reflection

"But I say to you, love your enemies, and pray for those who persecute you." These are pretty tough words to swallow. Jesus speaks clearly, however, about His expectation for us. It is really easy to love those who love and treat us well, but it is really hard to love those who hurt us. On a sheet of paper, write down the person(s) in your life who is the hardest to love. Tape the paper on your mirror so you are reminded to pray for this person when you wake up in the morning.

Prayer

Your love is perfect, Jesus. Take my heart and fill it with your perfect love. Teach me how to love and treat those I despise and those who have hated me with patience and kindness. Amen.

Exercise Three: Jesus Delivers Us from Our Fear

Matthew 8:23-27

Questions

1. Is your faith strong enough to step out of the boat?
2. What are some of the storms in your life this very moment? Has God helped you through some of these storms? If so, how?
3. Do you rely on God in times of fear?

Reflection

It's OK to worry, to be scared, and to feel fearful. But, it's important to remember: Fear is not from God. Fear has a tendency to take hold of us and consume us. If we constantly live in fear about things in our life, we will not be able to truly live as Christ wants us to. Many people worry about losing a loved one or not getting a job. They worry about their future, being lonely, being successful, or being a failure. It is normal to think about these things, but when fear steps in and begins to take over, it can paralyze us. Only Jesus can calm the storms and fears in our lives. What is your biggest fear? Allow God to give you the courage you need to face your fears.

Prayer

Jesus, help me see you amidst the "storms" in my life, that I may not be afraid of anything. I put my trust in you, my God. Deliver me from living in fear and grant me the courage to follow you. Amen.

Exercise Four: Jesus Delivers Us from Doubt

Matthew 16:15-20

Questions

1. Did you ever doubt that Jesus is truly the "Son of the living God," our "Savior"? Why did you doubt?
2. What can you do to ease or lessen the doubt you have in your faith?
3. Is having doubt about who God is good or bad? Why?

Reflection

Who do you say Jesus is? Do you truly believe He is the Messiah? There are times in our lives when we question and doubt our faith and belief in God. Even Peter, our first pope, denied Jesus. Peter quickly recognized his weakness, however, and began to pursue the Lord with a renewed vigor.

It's OK to be doubtful; if you weren't doubtful from time to time, you should worry. Turn doubt into an opportunity. Find out more about Jesus and your faith. Pursue Jesus with an open heart and learn all that you can about Him. Write down some of the questions you may have about God and your faith. Then find the answers by asking someone or looking them up yourself.

Prayer

Jesus, deliver me from doubting you and your love. Give me the eyes to see you working in my life. Give me a heart that is open to your truth and lead me into a deeper faith in you. Amen.

Exercise Five: Jesus Warns Us to be Ready

Matthew 25:1-13

Questions

1. When it's your time to enter the wedding feast (heaven) will Jesus say, "I know you" or "I do not know you"? Why?
2. Is it too late for you to prepare for the Kingdom of heaven? What can you do to prepare today?
3. What have you done this past week to make yourself one of the "wise" instead of one of the "foolish"?

Reflection

A lot of times you hear people say they'll "change after college" or "you've got to have fun now; worry later!" It has become a pretty popular idea that when you're a teenager, you can do whatever you want because you'll have plenty of time to straighten up or regain direction after college. Today, Jesus is reminding us that none of us know how long we're going to be here. He is challenging us to remain ready; which is to say, we should always try to act in a way that would make Jesus proud, in a way that will prepare us for heaven.

Prayer

I pray that you would give me the wisdom, Lord, to seek you first and not my own foolish desires. Prepare my heart, Jesus. Help me change my life for you now, not later. Transform my life so I will always be ready for you. Amen.

UNDERSTANDING MARK:
AN OVERVIEW WITH EXERCISES

"Maaaaaaaaaaaaaarrrrkkkk!" she shouted, letting all of our neighbors know that my presence was needed at home, immediately. I could always tell when my mother was worried about my whereabouts as she had the uncanny knack of turning my name — a one-syllable word — into a multi-syllable exclamation that would make even stray dogs flee.

It was in those moments that I was annoyed with my namesake, St. Mark, feeling as though I'd somehow lost out in the large Catholic family lotto for the best saint names. I mean, my older brothers could claim devil-slayers like St. Michael, snake-charmers like St. Patrick, and animal-tamers like St. Francis, just to name a few. And then there was me — stuck with good 'ol Mark, whose only endearing quality in my young, sarcastic mind was that he wrote the shortest Gospel.

It wasn't until my high school years that my eyes were opened to the gift my mother and father bestowed upon me in my name. A closer examination of the New Testament reveals that the author of the second Gospel was actually known as "John Mark" (Acts 12:25, 15:37). Though John was his Hebrew name, he became better known by his Roman name, Mark, and for good reason. Like the Greeks before them, the Romans had more gods than Cheesecake Factory has entrees. The Roman god of war was called Mars, of which "Mark" is a derivative. How blessedly different my early childhood would have been if someone would have clued me in on the fact that the name "Mark" — my name — translates to "mighty warrior."

Why, though, would the evangelist, who sought to spread the Good News, choose to go by his Roman name? Was it because he didn't want to be confused by the better known "John," the beloved disciple of Jesus? The answer actually has roots far deeper.

God designs each of us with a specific mission and Mark was no exception. The core audience Mark wrote to were Gentile (non-Jewish) Christians living in Rome. Inspired by the Holy Spirit, Mark's words would bring hope to Christians enduring persecution. Given this fact, it should come as no shock that Mark's portrait of Jesus is one of a wonder-working warrior, a perfect combination of divine power and mercy toward humanity. Put simply, if you can "understand" Mark's Gospel (which is the shortest and easiest), you will have the foundation needed to understand the other three and the remainder of the New Testament.

Several things make Mark's Gospel quite different than the others. You won't come across many long sermons in Mark's Gospel (there are only two, to be exact), nor will you find the "back story" of the nativity that you do in Matthew and Luke. In Mark, Jesus is a God of action, performing miracles and casting out demons at every drop of the hat and turn of the page. Mark's Gospel is fast-paced and power packed, which is one reason the symbol associated with Mark is the lion.

Through Mark's pen, the Holy Spirit breathes urgency into every chapter. Should you read the 16-chapter Gospel from start to finish, you'll notice that Mark uses the word "immediately" about 40 times. Note, too, that following Christ's Crucifixion, it is not a Jew or a regular Roman citizen but a high-ranking, Roman officer — a Centurion — who first proclaimed Christ's identity as the "Son of God" (15:39). Such a bold statement from a highly trained and revered soldier undoubtedly raised the eyebrows of more than a few in the Roman audience at the time.

Perhaps the passion and urgency communicated in Mark's account reflected as much about the author as they did about his Lord. One must wonder, however, where all this passion and intimate knowledge of Christ came from since Mark was not one of the original Twelve Apostles.

Mark was the cousin of St. Barnabas (Colossians 4:10), but it was his relationship with two other VIPs that gave him his credibility and information. Mark was a traveling companion to both St. Peter and St. Paul, offering him the best of both apostolic worlds. Peter obviously had a close relationship with the young evangelist, referring to him intimately as "my son Mark" (1 Peter 5:13). Mark's Gospel was obviously heavily influenced by the fisherman turned shepherd, Peter, offering eye witness details that could only be known by Peter, himself (4:35-38, 5:38-41). In fact, a closer examination of Peter's testimony in Acts 10:36-43 reveals an "outline" of sorts for Mark's entire Gospel.

Whether a scribe or recording secretary or merely a student with pristine memory, Mark's witness to the life of Christ was heavily influenced by Peter's "behind the scenes" eyewitness account. You'll notice that Mark doesn't just say, "they sat on the grass" but rather, "they sat down in groups of fifty on the green grass" (6:39). Jesus doesn't just fall asleep upon the boat but "asleep, in the stern, on a cushion" (4:38). Christ doesn't just calm the wind, he "rebukes" it (4:28). A large group doesn't just come to a house, "the entire town gathered" (1:33). Mark gives exact details about the possessed swine (5:13), the names of Simon of Cyrene's sons (15:21), and the healing commands of Jesus spoken in Aramaic (5:41, 7:34).

In Mark we are given the testimony of an eyewitness we can count on. Fast-paced, highly-detailed, short, and to the point, the Gospel of Mark is the "perfect place to start" if you're new to reading the Bible and want a jumping off point. Start with Mark and then you'll be ready to take on the other Gospels, too.

Exercise One: Jesus Delivers Us from Our Demons

Mark 5:1-13

Questions

1. Do you see yourself as good or bad? Why?
2. Do you believe God is more powerful than the evil in the world? Why or why not?
3. What can you do in your life to keep evil at a distance?

Reflection

It says in Scripture that "every knee shall bend and every tongue confess that Jesus Christ is Lord." Often times, we try to defeat demons in our life on our own and fail to realize that it cannot be done. We are totally helpless and outmatched. Jesus has healing power and authority over all things, and only with Jesus can we overcome the demons in our life. Do you have struggles? Are there things in your life you can't overcome? Are you weighed down by sin? Ask Jesus for help. He will always be there.

Prayer

Lord, I have made every attempt at breaking these chains that bind me and I now realize I cannot conquer the demons in my life on my own. Powerful God, deliver me from these demons; break these chains Lord, so that I may be free to live in your love. Amen.

Exercise Two: Jesus Reminds Us to Take Time to Pray

Mark 6:30-32

Questions

1. What is the purpose of prayer in your life? Is it for God, or for you?
2. Why did Jesus have the apostles go off by themselves to a deserted place and pray?
3. Is prayer a priority in your daily life? Why or why not?

Reflection

When do you pray? Do you only pray when you need something, or when things are going wrong and stress has taken over? Prayer is not all about asking for things; it's about communicating with Jesus on a regular basis. Prayer is our lifeline to God. We have to pick up the "phone" every day and spend time with Him. Whether it is five minutes or 30, we need to take time to be with Jesus. So, be consistent in your prayer and make it a priority in your daily life.

Prayer

Thank you, Jesus, for the gift of prayer. Help me take time to listen for your voice, to praise you for what you've done for me, to pray for your help, and to pray for others in need of your love. Amen.

Exercise Three: Jesus Reminds Us to be Children

Mark 10:13-16

Questions

1. What does it mean to be "childlike in our faith"?
2. Do you see yourself as being more "childlike" or "childish" when it comes to your faith? What is the difference?
3. Do you believe you are ready to enter the Kingdom of God, today? Why or why not?

Reflection

Do you have a lot of responsibilities or too many things to do, or do you constantly wish people would treat you more like an adult? Sometimes we need to just slow down and think back to when life was a little simpler. The innocence of a child is something to treasure. Children have such a simple yet sincere faith. You see, it's not until we get older that we begin to question things and turn away from our childlike faith. Allow the innocence of the child in you to be a part of your heart. Talk to your parents about things you did and said as a child or look at some old baby pictures. Get back in touch with your childhood. Remember, "whoever does not receive the kingdom of God like a child shall not enter it."

Prayer

Jesus, give me the innocence of a child. Help me run to you when I am hurt and laugh with you when I am joyful. Help me live a simple faith, always trusting and believing in you. Amen.

Exercise Four: Jesus Challenges Us to Tithe

Mark 10:17-31

Questions

1. Do you think it is harder for wealthy or poor people to enter heaven? Why?
2. What is more important to you, "treasure in heaven" or treasure on Earth? Why?
3. How do you give your time to Jesus?

Reflection

Do you tithe? To tithe is to give back to God what He has given us. As Christians, we are called to give ten percent of our income to the Church. Do you earn money but just count on your parents to contribute at church? Remember that you're a member of the Church, too. If you only get ten dollars a week, save one and give it to the Church. We should not only tithe our money, but our time. Do you take time to help others, serve the poor, help a friend in need, or help at your church? Give some of your time to Jesus. Trust that if you tithe, you will be blessed in many other ways.

Prayer

Thank you, Jesus. Thank you for the gift of your generous love. I pray that I can imitate your generosity, Lord, with my time and money. Help me give back to the Church and the poor. Save me from selfishness. I trust that you will honor my tithe Lord, and always give back more than what is given. Amen.

Exercise Five: Do an Act of Service

Mark 10:43-45

Questions

1. Do you view your daily tasks as service? Why or why not?
2. "In this life we cannot do great things. We can only do small things with great love" (Mother Teresa). What are some of these small things that can become acts of love?
3. How is God calling you to serve in your local community, home, and parish?

Reflection

Jesus came not to be served, but to serve. If we are to be Christians, followers of Christ, should we not imitate this? Admittedly, there are different types of service. We have to notice the crucial difference between serving others for the sake of getting a job done and serving others out of love. We are called to serve others not just when it suits us, but also when it's a true sacrifice. Loving and serving until it hurts is the lesson of the cross.

Think of the way a parent cares for their newborn baby. Night after night of very little sleep, a headache from the restless crying, sheer exhaustion. This kind of self-sacrificing, love-fueled service is what Christ is calling us to. It doesn't have to be a huge act of service, but rather the little things, the mundane, that are often the most difficult. The important thing to remember is to look at where your heart is. Are you serving as Christ would, out of love?

Go out of your way to serve someone today without seeking recognition or thanks.

Prayer

Jesus, help me to want to serve you every day. Help me see your face in those around me and know that by serving them with love, I am serving you. Help me recognize that with your help, I can do small things with great love. Amen.

UNDERSTANDING LUKE:
AN OVERVIEW WITH EXERCISES

A couple of years ago, my (then) fourth grade daughter spent time reading the Gospels before bed each night. This action was neither provoked nor forced on her by yours truly, yet the quality of her observations and the depth of the questions her sacred reading elicited on the mornings that followed were incredible.

She had questions about St. Luke and — more to the point — how he could be "trusted" as a source if he wasn't one of the original Twelve Apostles. I affirmed her observation and tried to quell her concerns by explaining that St. Luke was a convert to the faith and a close traveling companion of St. Paul.

"So, St. Luke *didn't really know* Jesus?" my daughter insightfully asked. Little did I know that on this particular morning I would introduce my now ten-year-old to the glory of sacred tradition.

Luke was not an eyewitness to Christ's works (Luke 1:2). He was the product of — and an eyewitness to — the *living tradition* (that St. Paul, Luke's mentor, speaks specifically about throughout his epistles). Luke's own conversion was due, in part, to Christ's command to carry the Gospel to the ends of the Earth (Matthew 28:20). Luke obviously benefited from this great charge — even writing about its Earth-changing effects in his own Acts of the Apostles (Acts 1:8, 17:6). And while Luke didn't "walk" with Jesus during His public ministry, it becomes clear through his writings that Luke most certainly *did know Him*.

Luke knew his audience, too. Since he was writing to non-Jews (Gentiles), he took time to translate any and all Hebrew or Aramaic (languages not as familiar to Gentiles) into Greek, the language they spoke. While making Christ's words and deeds accessible to this unique Gentile cross-section of readers and hearers, Luke also made it a point to champion the rights and dignity of the lowly and oppressed, placing women in high regard although they held a relatively low social status in the ancient Mediterranean world.

Consider what a special gift Luke is to the Church. Without the Holy Spirit breathing (inspiration) through Luke's pen, we would be without the Hail Mary or the joyful mysteries of the rosary, for you cannot have them without Luke's accounts of the Annunciation or visitation (and so on). We would, likewise, be without some of the most famous parables in history — the prodigal son (15:11-32) and the good Samaritan (10:25-37) to name but two. Consider the invitation to the shepherds at Christ's birth (2:8-12) or the angelic "Gloria" (2:14) we proclaim at every Mass -- again, made known to us through Luke. How about Jesus' boyhood misadventures, including when He went missing for three days (2:41-52)? Yep, that's Luke, too. Without Luke inclining his ear (and pen) to the Holy Spirit's inspiration, we would also be without the conversation between Martha and Mary (10:38-42), the raising of the widow's son at Nain (7:11-17), the dinner party with Zacchaeus (19:1-10), the exchange between Christ and the two thieves upon the cross (23:32-43), and the Resurrection story on the road to Emmaus (24:13-35), to name just a few.

In Luke's gorgeous work — his use of Greek is both highly educated and quite poetic — we are given a glimpse into Christ's mercy and compassion, as He is moved with pity and responds in kind to those most in need of the compassion only available in the Lord's sacred heart.

Exercise One: Pray a Rosary

Luke 1:41-45

Questions

1. What is your relationship like with Mary?
2. Do you find it easy to turn to her and ask for her intercession? Why or why not?
3. Have you ever been able to really reflect on the mysteries of the rosary? What mystery (joyful, sorrowful, glorious, or luminous) speaks to you the most at this time in your life?

Reflection

Mary, the perfect mother, is an amazing person to turn to. If you're happy asking friends, family, and others at church to pray for you, why not also turn to Mary with your prayer requests? What better person than Jesus' own mom to be praying for you and taking your burdens, worries, etc. to her Son! She has been and remains to be a perfect mother to turn to when we struggle with our own earthly mothers. She is a great example of humility, true beauty, grace, gentleness, and obedience. Mary, our beautiful and compassionate mother, keeps us wrapped tightly in her embrace; we should not be afraid to go to her and ask for her intercession when things begin to become too much for us to handle on our own.

Pray the rosary today. Far from a boring, repetitive prayer, the rosary gives us the opportunity to reflect on the life of Christ and seek the intercession of Mary.

It is a great prayer in times of distress, a great comfort and a great weapon. It is the weapon of Mary's' protection, the protection of a mother who can drive away anything that is keeping you from loving her Son fully and completely.

Prayer

Mother Mary, I ask for you to be present in my daily life, to intercede for me to your most precious Son. I pray that you may reveal some of the mysteries of the rosary to me and help me to pray the rosary, a gift of prayer you have blessed us with. May I come to know Christ through you. Amen.

Exercise Two: Jesus Faced Temptation

Luke 4:1-13

Questions

1. Do you have a hard time fighting temptation in your life? What temptation do you struggle with the most?
2. Temptation leads to sin. How does God help us fight the temptations the devil throws before us?
3. The Scripture passage says, "... when the devil had ended every temptation, he departed from him until an opportune time." What does that mean?

Reflection

Jesus was tempted just as we are, but Jesus resisted temptation and never gave in to Satan's antics. Jesus is our model for resisting temptation. We will always experience temptation, but we can resist any temptation with God's help. Saint Paul tells us in Philippians 4:13 that we "can accomplish all things through Christ, who strengthens us." Today, actively turn your back on temptation. Set some boundaries and don't be afraid to say, "no."

Prayer

Be with me, Jesus. In my times of temptation, hold me in your grace. Give me the strength to turn to you. I cannot avoid sin on my own, Lord. I am weak, but in your love, I am strong. In the name of Jesus, I rebuke the evil one. Amen.

Exercise Three: Jesus Delivers Us from Pain

Luke 8:43-48

Questions

1. Do you or someone you know suffer from a physical, emotional, or spiritual pain? How has this suffering impacted your faith in God?
2. In what ways does God heal our hurts, today?
3. Have you experienced the healing touch of God in your life? If so, how?

Reflection

Ask yourself this question, "Can God heal my pain?" You better believe He can. Jesus didn't just perform miracles back then; He also performs them today. What kind of pain do you have in your life? Do you have some deep hurts or wounds from things that happened in the past? Be open and honest with God about the pain in your life. Give Him a chance to heal you.

Prayer

Heal me, Jesus. Heal my heart if it is broken, my soul if it is weary, and my faith if it is weak. Deliver me from my pain, Lord, and bring me into the same joy that was felt by those you have healed throughout time. Amen.

Exercise Four: Jesus Reminds Us to Put Him First

Luke 10:38-42

Questions

1. Do you see yourself as being more like Martha or Mary? How so?
2. Is it better to be like Martha or Mary? Why?
3. What does it mean to put Christ first in your life?

Reflection

Many people think acts of service or other good things are all we need to do for Jesus. Although service is great, it's not the main priority of Jesus' "to-do" list. Are you like Martha or Mary? Both of these women had right intentions. However, Martha spent all of her time serving Jesus and forgot to spend time with Him. Mary enjoyed Jesus' company, knowing she would only have a little time with Him. So, who are you: Martha or Mary? Spend time with Jesus. Set aside some time throughout your day to pray and read Scripture. Go to your local adoration chapel or church and spend some time in front of the Blessed Sacrament.

Prayer

I put you first, Jesus. I put you above everything in my life: myself, my friends, my family, my schoolwork, my weekends, my desire for sin, my pride. Be my everything, Lord. Help me make you the first and last thing I think about. Amen.

Exercise Five: Jesus Remains with Us in the Eucharist

Luke 24:13-25

Questions

1. The lives of Jesus' apostles were changed following His death and Resurrection. How has Jesus' Resurrection affected your life?
2. Are you willing to allow Christ to be a part of your life and change it? If not, why? If so, how?
3. Do you believe Jesus is present in the Eucharist? Why or why not?

Reflection

This is one of the coolest passages in all of Scripture. It takes place after Jesus rose from the grave. The disciples never expected Him to rise, but Jesus did a lot of unexpected things. Jesus spent some time with the disciples before He ascended to heaven. The most awesome thing they did was celebrate the Eucharist together — the same Eucharist that we celebrate at every Mass. Jesus will always be present to us in the Eucharist. What a gift! Spend some time in front of the Blessed Sacrament. Reread the Scripture passage above. Reflect and journal on this awesome story.

Prayer

Thank you, Jesus. You are the Messiah, the Son of the living God. You are the king of all kings, the only true God. Thank you for the gift of the Eucharist. Give me eyes of faith that I may come to know and feel your awesome love in your body and blood. Give me a new respect and reverence for the Eucharist. Quiet my mind and heart when I am at Mass, so I may begin to understand the incredible mystery of the Eucharist. Amen.

UNDERSTANDING JOHN:
AN OVERVIEW WITH EXERCISES

I still recall my first Scripture class in college. The professor spent the entire class telling us how "dangerous" it is to study the Bible because it would destroy many of our preconceived (and immature) notions about Christ and His Church. "Most people," he maintained, "function from what their parents and pastors have told them about the *real Jesus* rather than what the text(s) actually say... and to do so is not only dangerous but woefully short-sighted." He invited us to shed the "water wings" and the "kiddie pool" of spoon-fed Biblical study, calling us into the deep of the synoptic Gospels.

By the end of the first class, I was ready to tear into my own, and often unopened, Bible. Exiting the class, however, it occurred to me to ask one glaring question, "Professor, why are we stopping with only the synoptics and not also studying the Gospel of John?"

He pointedly responded, "Ah, you must learn to swim before you attempt to scuba dive."

The response left me wanting to know more, so rather than completing my assigned reading in the synoptic Gospel, I read the entire Gospel of John in one sitting. Several passages of dialogue were confusing, and several details went right over my head — it was as though I was watching a foreign film with only sporadic subtitles. I knew nothing about John, his history nor the fact that he was most likely the "disciple whom Jesus loved."

Truthfully, I had no background to help me navigate this deep sea of God's grace that we call the fourth (and final) Gospel. My professor was right, this was like scuba diving and to experience the depths of the Holy Spirit's inspired brilliance, the average swimmer needs some training and tools to go deeper.

John is often referred to as "the beloved disciple" because he was Jesus' closest friend. The younger son of Zebedee, John was the one who rested upon Christ's chest at the Last Supper (John 21:20), the one entrusted with the ongoing care of Christ's mother, Mary, from the cross (John 19:25), and the only apostle not to die a martyr's death (John 21:20-23). Early traditions maintain, too, that following Pentecost, the Blessed Virgin Mary went to live with John in Ephesus, where he served as bishop.

Written for Jewish Christians, John's Gospel is filled with verses from the Old Testament. It was most likely written after the other Gospels, so he includes a lot of details left out by the others. John "fills in" some of the "gaps" by sharing unique stories and moments not previously recorded. Imagine for just a moment where we'd be without John's Gospel contribution! The wedding feast at Cana (2:1-11), the Samaritan woman at the well (4:1-43), the bread of life discourse (6:25-69), the raising of Lazarus (11:17-44), the washing of the feet (13:1-17), the extended dialogue with Pilate (18:28-19:16), the episode with Mary and John at the cross (19:25-27), and the Resurrection appearance on the Sea of Tiberias (21:1-25) are but a few gorgeous passages we would not have if the Spirit hadn't breathed through John's blessed pen.

John emphasizes the fact that Jesus was not "just another guy." Christ was both God and man. God became man so that human beings could live with Him in heaven. God created the world in Genesis and now Jesus is working a new "spiritual creation" in the lives of His followers. His entire Gospel is highly symbolic, rooted in the Old Covenant all the while pointing toward the New. It is only when we comprehend the dual nature of Christ (human and divine) that we can come to comprehend the purpose of His mission and the glory of the Church He instituted on Earth.

John's Gospel is a constant invitation to advance forward from "simple" reading and plunge into the sacramental waters. For John, everything points us back to the Church and her sacraments. Different types of Biblical writing try to accomplish different things. John, however, weaves together both the symbolic and historical into an unprecedented and gorgeous tapestry of faith. The fourth Gospel is much like an iceberg, where 90 percent of its greatness is below the surface.

If Mark's gospel is considered the "easiest," John's is the deepest. It will immerse you into the Church's tradition by inviting you ever deeper into the heart of the sacraments. It will offer you a glimpse at the one who came with power and purpose, at the appointed time, to save us from our sins and from ourselves. John calls us into the deep waters for a scuba dive once we are comfortable "getting out of the boat" in the synoptic Gospels.

Exercise One: Jesus Got Angry

John 2:13-16

Questions

1. Does it surprise you that Jesus got so angry? Why?
2. Do you see your body as a "temple of the Holy Spirit," a place where the Holy Spirit lives? Does Jesus get angry when we abuse our bodies?
3. What were the people doing in the Father's house? Was Jesus angrier with the people or with their actions?

Reflection

Yes, even Jesus got angry. However, Jesus' anger was justified. He was defending His Father and rebuking the fact that people were disrespectful to God's house. When you get angry, is your anger justified? Does your anger lead to sin and cause hurt? Make peace with someone you have gotten angry with and ask them for forgiveness. If your anger has caused you to sin, ask for forgiveness in the Sacrament of Reconciliation.

Prayer

Have mercy on me, Jesus. Forgive me if I've angered you by abusing myself or others, or if my desire for material things has become a god in my life. Lord, help me seek forgiveness from those I have angered and those who have angered me. Help me give others the same mercy you have given me. Amen.

Exercise Two: *Jesus is the Bread of Life*

John 6:53-58

Questions

1. Do you believe Jesus is fully present in the Eucharist? Why or why not?
2. How can you prepare your heart to receive Christ in the Eucharist?
3. What sacrifices would you need to make in order to attend daily Mass? Are you willing to make them?

Reflection

When we receive the Eucharist, we are receiving Jesus into our bodies and our hearts. Our bodies, already holy because of the Holy Spirit living in us, become a living tabernacle when we receive the Eucharist. What an amazing gift — Christ giving Himself to us — and what a fantastic opportunity to be able to receive Christ in this way, daily. Not only are we in union (becoming one) with Christ, we are also in communion with the entire "body of Christ" throughout the world. What a great sense of community formed by sharing in this gift of Christ with each practicing Catholic throughout the world! Christ, the life-giving bread, gives us the opportunity to draw life from Him, who is the fullness of life. Who wouldn't want a share in this life?

Prayer

Thank you, Lord, for sacrificing your physical body so that you could become my spiritual food and drink. You are true, life-giving bread for me. Thank you for the gift of your Church and the gift of the Eucharist. Help me to more fully participate in the celebration of the Eucharist and have the zeal to want to seek you, daily. Amen.

Exercise Three: Jesus Shows Us Compassion

John 8:2-11

Questions

1. When you sin, who condemns you more? Your friends, your parents, yourself, or God?
2. Are you hesitant or afraid to go to the Sacrament of Reconciliation? Why?
3. Have you ever reflected on your own sinful ways after you judged someone else for theirs? What was that experience like?

Reflection

This Scripture passage offers us two challenges: to forgive and not to judge. Both are tough to overcome, but they're what Jesus is calling us to do and not to do. Is there someone in your life you have judged? Go to that person and ask for forgiveness. Is there someone in your life who has judged you, or who you need to forgive? Go to that person and forgive them.

Prayer

Jesus, help me see my own sinfulness before the sins of others. Show me your compassion, Lord, and take away any fear I have of the Sacrament of Reconciliation. Make me worthy of your mercy, Jesus. Amen.

Exercise Four: Jesus Delivers Us from Death

John 11:30-44

Questions

1. Do you see God as a compassionate God or a punishing God? Why do you see Him this way?
2. Why did Jesus raise Lazarus from the dead?
3. Do you believe God can transform your life? If so, which parts of your life?

Reflection

Does death scare you? It is our hope as Christians that when we die we will share eternal life with Jesus and the saints. The catch is that we can't be spiritually dead here on Earth. It's time to rise up. Jesus is saying to all of us that He is the answer to spiritual death, and like Lazarus, Jesus is calling us out of the tomb. Are you dead in your faith? Is your spiritual life non-existent or struggling? Jesus is calling you out of the tomb to experience a new life in Him. Wake up, come out, and embrace life. Give someone a smile or a hug today and when you do, remind yourself of the importance of living each day to its fullest.

Prayer

Thank you, Lord, for the gift of life. Give me the grace to live my life for you completely. Awaken my heart if it is numb or dead; fill it with faith and passion for you. Amen.

Exercise Five: Jesus Calls Us to Serve One Another

John 13:3-9

Questions

1. Do you see yourself as being more of a foot washer (servant), or someone who has your feet washed (being served)?
2. Give two examples of "foot washers" who have affected your life.
3. What are ways in which you can be a foot washer to others?

Reflection

Why would Jesus ever want to wash the feet of the disciples? Why would God want to deal with dirty, sweaty feet? "Christ did not come to be served, but to serve." Jesus knew serving God meant serving others. Serving can be tough because it means putting others' needs before our own. Clean your room and your house. Don't wait for your parents to ask you to do it. Maybe even clean out your closet and give some of your clothes to the needy.

Prayer

Lord God who created everything, you came to this Earth in human form to serve. Change my heart into that of a servant's heart. May I do good for others and expect nothing in return. When my pride gets in the way, Lord, remind me of how you washed your disciples' feet and served those in need. Nothing is beyond you, Lord. Thank you, Jesus. Amen.

THE MAIN EVENTS OF THE GOSPELS

Most people in the modern world have heard some part of the story of Jesus Christ. Even if they cannot tell you that the angel's name was Gabriel or that you can read about the angel's appearance to the Blessed Virgin Mary in **Luke 1**, they probably know bits and pieces of the story. Perhaps they know, too, about Joseph's powerful dreams (**Matthew 1**) or the angelic revelation to the shepherds (**Luke 2**) or the Magi following the star (**Matthew 2**).

You might not even know all the "wheres" these stories are found (as in which Gospel or chapter), but you likely know many of the details of Jesus' life. See how many of the following stories you recognize — these *major events* of the Gospels — and feel free to read any of them again or for the first time.

Not long after the magi's visit, the homicidal King Herod seeks to have the baby Jesus killed. As the holy family escapes to Egypt, they "disappear" for several years, at some point returning to Nazareth and to St. Joseph's trade as a carpenter/stone worker. Jesus appears, again, at the age of 12 (**Luke 2**) when He goes missing from the family caravan following their observance of Passover in the city of Jerusalem (which was 90 miles away from home and a multiple day trip). Following this episode, we don't really hear from Jesus again until He prepares to begin His public ministry.

Following Jesus' baptism in the River Jordan (**Mark 1**), He is thrust out into the wilderness where He prays and fasts for 40 days and nights. It is here that the devil tempts and tries Jesus (**Matthew 4**) and we see the Lord defeat him handily, using only Scripture as His defense. We see Jesus meet and call His first disciples (**John 1, Luke 5**) and perform His first public miracle at the Wedding at Cana (**John 2**).

It quickly becomes clear this is no mere "small-town carpenter" as Jesus' fame spreads throughout Galilee (northern Israel) and Judea (southern Israel). Jesus scandalized people with His love for the outcast (**Luke 5**), sinners (**John 8, Luke 19**), and even the Samaritans (**John 4**), a group the Jews greatly despised. He makes a name for Himself curing the lame (**Matthew 9**), healing the blind (**John 9**), and restoring the lepers (**Luke 17**). Thousands watched and were fed as Jesus multiplied loaves and fish to feed the masses (**John 6**). The apostles watched Him walk on water (**Matthew 14**), raise the dead (**Mark 5, John 11**), and be transfigured before their very eyes (**Matthew 17**). Not only did this rabbi claim to have insights into the eternal, He actually claimed to be divine — to be one with the living God (**John 10**). This audacious claim demanded a verdict that Jesus actually backed up with signs, wonders, and miracles the likes of which no one had ever seen. He made prophecies and assertions no one had ever made, losing many followers because of the audacity that His flesh and blood would become literal food and drink we must receive "if we want to have life within us" (**John 6**).

His sermons (**Matthew 5**) lift the hearts of the lowly and oppressed, speaking of the Kingdom of God that was now at hand (**Luke 4**). People began to believe that Christ was the long-awaited Savior — the Messiah —

and rumors spread as to what that meant to the Israelite people. They believed He would overthrow their Roman oppressors and instill a new system of government and power (**Luke 9**, **Luke 24**). The Pharisees and Sadducees (the reigning Jewish religious leaders) were threatened by Christ's popularity and influence and began to see Him as a threat (**Matthew 12**) and not merely a harmless, unconventional rabbi.

After roughly three years of a very public ministry and after instituting a visible "head" to the apostles (**Matthew 16**) and a hierarchy to carry out His teachings, Jesus' earthly mission had fulfilled its purpose (**Matthew 28**). As His influence became too much for His opponents to bear, one of His closest followers would betray Him to His enemies.

Christ and His followers went to Jerusalem to honor the high and great feast of Passover as they no doubt did every year. As He entered the city, His followers greeted Him with chants of praise and laid down palm fronds at the feet of His donkey on a day we commemorate as Palm Sunday (**Luke 19**). As the (holy) week progressed, Jesus was tested by His adversaries as they tried to trap Him (**Matthew 22-25**) and find a charge to bring against Him.

Then, on what we call Holy Thursday, Jesus took the Twelve Apostles into an upper room of a house in the city (**Luke 22**). He washed their feet (**John 13**) as a sign of His selfless and sacrificial heart, an act of humility and service that would serve as the foundation for all who call themselves disciples of Jesus Christ. Next, He took common bread and wine, blessed it, broke it, and gave it to them, only this Passover meal was different (**Matthew 26, Luke 22**). Through His priestly prayer, Christ instituted the Eucharist, transforming (transubstantiating, actually) the bread and wine into His own body and blood. His prophecy would now be fulfilled as He ushered in and created a new priesthood. The sacrifice of self He offered in the upper room was the first act — for just as He offered us His body and blood on the altar of the wooden table, less than a day later He would offer us this divine gift upon the wood of the cross!

He retreated to the Garden of Gethsemane to pray before the betrayer, Judas Iscariot, arrived with soldiers to arrest Him (**Matthew 26, John 18**). The apostles scattered. Jesus was abandoned, given an unfair trial under the veil of night at the house of the high priest, Caiaphas (**Matthew 26**), and then remanded to King Herod Antipas (the figurehead ruler) and, eventually, to the Roman governor, Pontius Pilate (**John 19**). Though innocent, Christ was flogged and scourged at the pillar (**Matthew 27**). He was brazenly mocked with a crown of thorns and tortured within an inch of His life (**Mark 15**). Though Pilate wanted to release Him, the politician bowed to the pressure of the crowds (**John 18**) and sent Christ to His death on the cross.

After carrying His cross beyond the city walls, Jesus was nailed to it and executed between two common thieves at Golgotha, also known as Calvary (**Matthew 27, John 19**). Upon the cross, Christ demonstrated perfect love and fidelity, forgiving His persecutors and reconciling one of the thieves to God the Father (**Luke 23**). As Jesus breathed His last breath, the Earth shook and the sky fell dark (**Mark 15**, **Luke 23**). Creation killed its creator. Once taken down, the Lord was placed in a borrowed tomb, with a boulder enclosing it and a Roman guard stationed outside (**Matthew 27**). On the following Sunday morning, Mary Magdalene and a group of women were heading to the tomb to anoint the body when they noticed the stone moved and the body gone (**Matthew 28**, **John 20**). After a vision of the risen Lord, Mary Magdalene went to share the miraculous news with the apostles in hiding. Two of the apostles went and found the empty tomb but no body (**John 20**). Later that day, the glorified and risen Jesus passed through locked doors and stood in their midst (**John 20**). He came in peace and joy. He gave them a new mission and physically appeared to them several times over the next 40 days (**John 21**). At that time, He ascended (**Matthew 28**, **Luke 24**, **Acts 1**) bodily into heaven and promised them the Holy Spirit, which descended in power at Pentecost ten days later.

The Gospel message spread and the Church grew, first by hundreds and then by thousands. There are over one billion Catholics in the world today and hundreds of millions of Christians of various denominations, all of whom have these Gospel stories in common.

Take some time to read them with your own eyes and ask the Holy Spirit to help them come to life as you do.